Not A Partnership

www.NotAPartnership.com

Copyright © 2019
by Tod Jacobs and Peter Lynn

ISBN (hardcover edition) 978-0-578-44864-0
ISBN (paperback edition) 978-0-578-42913-7

All rights reserved.
No part of this publication may be translated, reproduced, stored in a retrieval system or transmitted, in any form or by any means, electronic, mechanical, photocopying, recording, or otherwise, without permission in writing from the author.
The rights of the copyright holder will be strictly enforced.

10   9   8   7   6   5   4   3   2   1

Not A Partnership

TOD JACOBS & PETER LYNN

Why We Keep Getting Marriage Wrong,
& How We Can Get It Right

Dedicated to
Mariam Jacobs
and
Regine Lynn
*our beloved wives
who have shown us what it means
to be a truly loving spouse.*

Contents

Prologue.................9
Introduction..............15

PART ONE
What Exactly is Marriage and Why is it So Important?

- 27 Back to the Beginning: What is Marriage?
- 41 Biology, Emotion & Soul
- 53 Giving

PART TWO
The Four Pillars of Giving

- 83 Overview of the Four Pillars
- 89 PILLAR #1: Keep it Fresh!
- 143 PILLAR #2: Gratitude: Feel It & Show It!
- 169 PILLAR #3: Respect in All Its Forms
- 203 PILLAR #4: It All Depends On Me

Conclusion...............223
Acknowledgments.........225

Prologue

THIS BOOK WAS BORN in 2016 in a cafe on the Upper West Side of Manhattan. I was sitting with Yuval, an alumnus from the post-graduate program I co-founded, and where Peter and I have taught since 2005. Yuval — late 20s, talented, socially adept, heart of gold — was about mid-way through his second year of marriage. "Why is it," Yuval asked, "that marriage is so hard? We love each other, we're attracted to each other, we have similar values — but we often fight, and we always seem to be questioning the future of the relationship. Why can't we get it right?!"

I thought about it for a moment. "It's because you don't understand what marriage *is*," I answered. "You don't know how to define it. And if you can't define it, don't know what a healthy one looks like, and don't know your goal, how can you expect to get it right?"

The student pushed back: "What do you mean? What am I missing?"

I thought back to a sharp piece of wisdom I'd heard years earlier from a well-known South African rabbi[1] and replied: "You think that marriage is a partnership. You have

---

1. Dr. Akiva Tatz.

your rights and obligations, and I have my rights and obligations. So, like most partners, I spend my time convinced that I'm doing my job perfectly, but always disappointed in her for not holding up her end of the bargain. And of course she's making the exact same set of assumptions from her end. My dear, *marriage is not a partnership*."

Yuval sat stunned for a few moments. "You *have* to write a book on marriage, with exactly that title!" he exclaimed. He then thought for another moment and asked, "So...if it's not a partnership, what *is* it?"

That question led to a fruitful discussion with Yuval about what marriage is, and how it works. That marriage, above all, is life's greatest platform for constant giving. That a husband or wife can take full responsibility for making the relationship work and for making the other happy, irrespective of whether the spouse is giving in kind. That great marriages are *made*, not received. I tried to paint a picture in which a husband and wife view their ultimate role as acting the way that the *spouse* needs. And how, ultimately, when we approach marriage in this way, we can generate a lifetime of happiness and wellbeing, literally becoming one with our soulmate.

After that conversation I phoned Peter Lynn and suggested that we write a book together. Since 2005, Peter has partnered with me in a post-graduate study program that, post my Wall Street career, I co-founded in Jerusalem. The David Robinson Institute for Jewish Heritage brings together gifted and idealistic young men with leadership qualities who wish to spend a year or two immersed in not only classical Jewish legal and philosophical texts, but in the intensive study of character and relationships as well. The aim? To prepare these future businessmen, doctors, lawyers, artists and teachers to successfully juggle life's great challenges of career, marriage, raising children, community leadership and spiritual growth.

Since that time, we and our colleagues have helped hundreds of young men develop their potential and become people of personal integrity, greatness, and stature. In that work, Peter has proven a critical resource to our students and alumni, combining real-world experience, phenomenal intuitive knowledge of people and relationships, and formal training in Positive Psychology at the University of Pennsylvania. Together, we have spent many hours teaching our students the theory behind building a great marriage, and countless more hours in the trenches with these young couples, counseling them as they grapple with the real-life challenges and promises of married life.

This book is the culmination of decades spent integrating powerful and ancient Talmudic and Kabbalistic wisdom with the real-life, real-time dramas being played out in the married lives of our students.

Year after year, we see that for even the most sophisticated and accomplished men and women — some of whom have been married for years — basic questions about marriage have gone unanswered and, shockingly, mostly unasked:

- What exactly is a marriage?
- Beyond the somewhat outdated traditional justifications of financial and physical security, or a desire to

raise kids in a stable setting, is there any deeper purpose in creating a legal framework for our relationship?
- Isn't a series of great romances and intimate encounters preferable to a lifelong commitment to a single person?
- Even if this person seems worth committing myself to *now* — what happens when things change? What if an illness arises, and I have to assume the role of caretaker? What if the money we expected to materialize simply doesn't? What happens when the good looks start to fade? In short: Why stay married if it's no longer good for me and surely not what I initially bought into?
- Why take the risk, given the rather daunting odds of failure?
- What does a healthy marriage look like?
- Can a person in this generation — where there are few successful role models — navigate marriage based upon little more than gut instincts? Would she do that with her career? Would he do that even with his diet and exercise program? The contrast would be humorous if it weren't so terrifying in its implications.

Somehow, when it comes to marriage — possibly life's most challenging endeavor — we enter with literally no preparation. No training, no instruction manual, no clear vision of the goal or pathway. Sometimes we have little more than a vague set of expectations derived from a lifetime of novels and Hollywood fantasies about love and romance (all of which *end* with the young couple falling madly in love, just as the curtain should in fact *rise* on the real work of building a marriage).

In the chapters that follow, we have attempted to define what marriage is — *and what it isn't* — and then to lay out practical steps that can bring the theory to life. Properly done with care, thought, tenacity, and above all, giving, we can transform marriage into a living source for the love, warmth, security and sense of wholeness that we crave and deserve.

Tod Jacobs
Jerusalem 2019

Introduction

WHY READ A BOOK ON MARRIAGE?
In the world of marriage, the stakes could not be higher — or more risky. On the one hand, most of us view marriage as one of the most critical aspects of our lives. More than 60% of unmarried people want to marry,[2] and by the age of 45, about 90% of people have been married.[3] Indeed, one of the greatest regrets expressed by patients in palliative care, close to death, is that they wished they had spent more of their time and energy with their spouse and children.[4] Most of us constantly hear from our friends and colleagues that marriage is the most important thing in life and commands the highest priority.

At the same time, the odds of successful marriage are stacked against us. To quote the Census Bureau's pithy summary: "Nearly everyone marries," but "nearly half of recent

---

2. Cohn, D'vera. "Love and Marriage." *Pew Research Center*. February 13, 2013, www.pewsocialtrends.org/2013/02/13/love-and-marriage.
3. Cohn, D'vera.
4. Ware, Bronnie. *The Top Five Regrets of the Dying*: A Life Transformed by the Dearly Departing. Carlsbad: Hay House Inc., 2012.

first marriages may end in divorce."[5] Somehow, despite the critical importance we ascribe to marriage and its place in our lives, we usually fail.

The issues that give rise to marital problems are as many and manifold as the people who experience them. But there are two causes for almost all failed and failing marriages.

First, we pay lip service to the critical nature of the institution without actually investing anywhere near the same amount of time and effort that we invest in other important parts of our lives, like career, health, and other interests. In my career, it's a given that I have to prepare thoroughly, work hard, subject myself to review, always look and act my best, stay current on all information and wisdom related to my job, and frankly, stop at nothing to make sure I succeed. But when it comes to my marriage, I spend precious little energy preparing and seeking to understand what it is and how I can best function as a successful and ever-better spouse. By the time we are *forced* to invest time in marriage, it's usually too late, after much damage has been done, and this investment is almost solely in the form of therapy or self-help books and materials. In short, we spend little time before the wedding preparing to succeed, and lots of time after the wedding struggling to fix where we have failed.

Second, even if we are willing to make the investment, we simply lack clarity in what the true goal of marriage is,

---

5. Kreider, Rose M., and Jason M. Fields. "Number, Timing, and Duration of Marriages and Divorces: Fall 1996." *Current Population Reports*, p. 70-80. U.S. Census Bureau, Washington, DC, www.census.gov/prod/2002pubs/p70-80.pdf.

what a beautiful marriage looks like, and how marriage is meant to function. Lacking a clear goal we are even more befuddled about how to get there. In virtually every other arena in which we seek greatness, the pathway is known or can be discovered. If I want to be a doctor, I go to medical school and learn the curriculum. If I want to play piano like a master, I hire a teacher and practice for hours every day to improve my technique. But when it comes to marriage, the goal becomes fuzzy. I want a good and happy marriage, but how do I get there? Perhaps I have never even seen a great marriage before. Even if I have been lucky enough to see a good marriage, navigating that path myself, even with a willing spouse, often proves elusive. There are too few talented jungle guides to lead me there. I don't even know where "there" is.

WHAT THE DICKENS HAPPENED TO MY GREAT EXPECTATIONS?

The *tragedy* of uninformed marriage lies not just in the high failure rate, but more precisely in the gulf between the lifelong expectation of the deep happiness and fulfillment that the relationship will provide, and the sad reality of what marriage really looks like, even if it survives. Bad outcomes are painful, but they are excruciating when the hopes were so high.

In the words of one Harvard researcher: "It's not marriage that makes you happy, it's a happy marriage that makes you happy."[6]

---

6. Munsey, Christopher. "Does Marriage Make Us Happy?" *Monitor on Psychology*, American Psychological Association. October, 2010, www.apa.org/monitor/2010/10/marriage.aspx.

It is no surprise, then, that hopeful, but often frustrated, confused or unhappy spouses have spawned an exploding industry of marriage books, seminars, therapy, and coaching.

The brilliant economists, Steven D. Levitt and Stephen J. Dubner, note in a different context (child raising), "In our society, if someone wants to be a hairstylist or a kickboxer or a hunting guide — or a schoolteacher — he or she must be trained and licensed by a state agency. No such requirement is necessary for parenthood."[7] Even less is expected and required for entry into marriage. Honestly, how do we stand a chance?

Why this book?

Is *another* book on marriage really needed?

We're busy. You're busy. It is truly hard to keep spending more and more time working on my relationship. So why should we spend time writing, and you reading (let alone buying), *another* book on marriage?

To make matters worse, there are lots of great books on marriage that we, like you, have read and found insightful and helpful. The powerful revelations regarding the fundamental differences between men and women by authors like Carol Gilligan and Deborah Tannen have had a quarter of a century to percolate through the collective psyche. Books like *Men are from Mars, Women are from Venus* and *The Five Love Languages* have given us tools and practical steps to integrate into our daily lives to enhance how

---

[7]. Levitt, Steven D. and Stephen J. Dubner. *Think Like a Freak: the Authors of Freakonomics Offer to Retrain Your Brain*. New York: William Morrow, 2014.

we communicate with, give to, receive from, and love our spouses. These books are amazing, helpful, and powerful. We have read many of them and we want you to read them.

So, again, what's the point of *this* book?

This book is different from all other books. All other books give us tips and advice about how to *be* married and what *to do* in marriage.

This book *defines* marriage.

What we present herein is the prerequisite for the other marriage books, because in order to get the most out of all the wonderful contemporary works on marriage, we first need to understand what marriage actually *is*.

Most marriage books assume that the reader already knows what marriage is and what it should be. After all, a person reading a book about marriage is probably already married or planning to get married, so of course he or she must know what marriage is. And even if we cannot quite express it in words, we have Google to define it for us:

> **Mar·riage** *(n)*: the legally or formally recognized union of two people as partners in a personal relationship (historically and in some jurisdictions specifically a union between a man and a woman).

To put it mildly, this definition is vague, superficial, and not terribly helpful. Barring the legal point in parentheses, it could just as easily describe my relationship with a close friend.

How fascinating is it that people yearn and dream for marriage, suffer through failed and sometimes hurtful relationships to find "the one," make that "til death do us part" commitment — and then discover they are not quite sure how to define exactly what it is that they have been yearning and struggling for. We pick up a junior high school level definition, and we're good to go!

TREATING THE SYMPTOMS AND IGNORING THE DISEASE

As problems arise in our marriages we seek solutions, but we often get stuck at the surface level. In the medical profession, the difference between a great doctor and a mediocre one often comes down to how they treat an illness. The inexperienced practitioner spends lots of time treating symptoms. While that approach may help the patient feel better, as long as the infection at the root level is left untreated it will continue to fester and eventually overwhelm the salves and painkillers. It becomes far more difficult to treat, as undiagnosed or ignored problems tend to worsen over time. The understanding healer always works on the root cause of the pathology. It may be more complicated and often more painful, but it brings true healing.

Our lack of a clear definition and clear goals of a healthy marriage not only prevent us from addressing underlying issues, but also leave us highly susceptible to burnout. When our marriage is missing a unifying and galvanizing theme, all those randomly acquired pieces of advice and good tips eventually become haphazard, confusing, and overwhelming. Without a clear picture of the destination, even the most sophisticated GPS — with all of its real-time data and knowledge of shortcuts and roadblocks and hazards — will fail, unless the goal is to get nowhere fast.

LET'S FIGURE OUT WHERE WE'RE GOING

Why this book? Because *we know the definition of marriage and want to share it with you!* In the ensuing chapters we will define not only the goal, but time-tested means of helping you get there.

The definition of marriage, together with its practical application, that we will present in this book is drawn from numerous sources. We'll dive into the oldest and, quite amazingly, most insightful source we have yet found — the Book of Genesis — for a glimpse into what marriage is all about, what it's meant to achieve, and why it's worth the struggle above all other pursuits. We'll marry that up, pun intended, with cutting-edge research on relationships. And we'll discuss practical steps to becoming great spouses, friends, and lovers. The goal is nothing less — and don't settle for less! — than to produce a great and enduring relationship that will form the core pleasure, meaning, and security amidst our tumultuous lives. The extensive experience of the authors in preparing our students for marriage and in counseling them along the way adds the real-world dimension to the theoretical framework.

While some of the source material is "spiritual," the insights contained therein are by no means confined to religious adherents. Indeed, the power of the ideas lies in their universality and self-evident depth and truth. Whatever your background and beliefs may be, we believe that the ideas speak for themselves and have proven themselves unequivocally powerful and compelling across the centuries.

In summary, we've divided the book into two parts:
1. What is a great marriage?
2. How can I have one?

OBJECTIVE #1: KNOW THE THEORY

This book begins with the premise that while we may recognize many fundamental truths about marriage and we may have learned some helpful tactics, we nonetheless remain at a loss when it comes to truly understanding many key aspects of marriage, such as:

- *What* a marriage really is
- *Why* we need (and desire) marriage
- *What* the goals of marriage are
- *Why* it is that men and women function so differently
- *How* the fundamental responsibilities of a spouse are defined
- *What* a truly healthy relationship even looks like
- **And most importantly**, *what key elements* make a marriage work (let alone thrive).

Our first objective, then, is to answer these questions. As we will show, with proper vision and a willingness to invest, two people who could not be more different from each other can attain a transformational unity between them that far surpasses what either one could achieve alone.

The process of focused and continual giving to each other can produce not only a great marriage — and a nurturing environment for children, physical security and financial benefit. That very process can and will help produce two great individuals as well. Giving enobles and expands us. The more you place on your shoulders, the greater your stature becomes.

If completion as a human being is what you seek, marriage is the vehicle that can get you there.

CRUSHING THE HARMFUL MARITAL MYTHS

In order to answer the key question of what marriage *is*, we must clarify what it *isn't*. There are some key myths and false premises we absorb throughout life that ironically work to uproot and destroy the very institution they seek to embrace:

- It's easy since we're in love
- I can wing it
- Marriage is romance
- Romance is love
- Romance lasts forever
- My gosh, we're so different. We must have made a mistake in marrying in the first place
- Marriage is a partnership
- I'll love my spouse when he starts loving me
- I'll give to her once she starts giving to me
- Maybe changing the definition or structure of marriage will save us
- Maybe two master bedrooms will foster peace at home

- Maybe "open marriage" — inviting others into our bedrooms (with my spouse's permission!) — will help ensure our ability to remain happily married

The list goes on and on....

OBJECTIVE #2: MAKE IT HAPPEN!

Once we've clearly defined marriage and its goals, we'll turn to Part 2 in order to lay out the key elements that will help us transform the theoretical picture into a real and flourishing marriage. We have divided the practical steps towards building your marriage into four golden pillars of activity and investment:

- Keep it fresh
- Gratitude: feel it and show it
- Respect in all its forms
- Responsibility: it all depends upon me!

IF NOT NOW, WHEN?

Let's begin the process of integrating our ideas with our actions. If marriage is as high a priority as we claim, let's start the work today, here and now, by taking the mission critical step of defining what a healthy and happy marriage actually is.

PART ONE

What Exactly is Marriage and Why is it So Important?

Back to the Beginning: What is Marriage?

TAKING SIDES

Before we learn how to apply research, experience, and wisdom as guides to marriage, let's take a journey back to the beginning. The essential answers to the questions of *what* marriage is and *why* marriage is can be found in the world's oldest book, in its description of the very first marriage in the history of man. At the peak of the process of building the world, the Creator made Adam and Eve. A closer look at the story will reveal something quite astonishing. When Genesis[8] describes the making of man, the verse states that *"male and female He created them."* The first human being was, quite literally, a unified person who was *both male and female*.

The English word "Adam" fails to capture the nuance of the original Hebrew. The Hebrew word "Adam" is not a

---

8. Genesis 1:27.

proper name, nor does it translate as "male." "Adam" simply means *human*. In fact, it is not until a full chapter later that "God cast a deep sleep upon the human...and He took one of his sides and...fashioned the side that He had taken from the human into a woman."[9] Ultimately, and for some reason (as we'll see), the two parts of the original human entity needed to be separated into two individual and different beings, man and woman. With Eve removed from Adam, each part was left with a certain lack that only the other would be able to fill. Adam, from whom an essential part had been removed, was left incomplete. Eve, created from a part of the original person, was left incomplete. They became two physical beings, each lacking an emotional and spiritual piece held by the other. Yet those two physical beings were first created as one.

ONE TO TWO TO ONE

Now, assuming that the Almighty knows what He's doing, what on earth was the point of creating the first human as a male-female if the point was to separate them forever after? The answer has compelling implications: Man and woman were initially an undivided, unified entity. Totally one. Nothing separated them. Their understanding and sensitivities were exactly the same. Their physical, emotional, and spiritual ideals and goals and desires aligned perfectly. They could effortlessly produce children and navigate life in the Garden of Eden without any conflict. One team from start to finish. A marriage made in heaven.

But that original oneness of man and wife was given

---
9. Genesis 2:21-22.

only as a short and temporary gift, a sort of spiritual template or paradigm that would forever echo in the human soul. Yes, we are now created separate, alone, unique in our understandings and desires and ideals. But our separateness comes with the deep subconscious realization that alone we're simply not whole. By ourselves we feel like half a human. We don't belong alone. We crave fulfillment. We seek intimacy. We long to trust and count on someone, and to be that person upon whom the other can always rely. We therefore have to look beyond ourselves to *re*-establish that greater unity. That's the true source of our aching and longing for a deep and intimate relationship with an *other*. It's not just about fulfilling our physical drives. It's not just about having children. It's about becoming whole again. Our own re-enactment of the Adam and Eve marriage.

The beauty of marrying and building a relationship is an echo of that original oneness and our soul-level desire to restore it. Together we can build and complete each other into something far greater than either of us could achieve by ourselves. Scripture could not have stated that goal more clearly: *They shall become one flesh.*[10] This, above all else, forms the powerful longing to marry which most of us experience.

Taking Alone

This leads to a perplexing question: If the goal is unity, why did the Almighty separate man and woman in the first place?

The answer starts with an insight. Alone and self-sufficient, we tend to burn out as human beings. For a time, we

---
10. Genesis 2:24.

revel in our independence. When a baby can hold the spoon herself, when she takes those first glorious steps, as she frees herself from her parents' grip, as she begins to make a living and support herself, the feeling is just amazing — the exhilaration of becoming "me"!

But at some point, that independence starts to give way to self-centeredness and self-absorption. I like it my way. I want my things just so. I want this furniture and this music and that movie and this food and the other vacation. Remember Burger King's old jingle, "Have It Your Way"? (It was surpassed only by Burger King's updated motto, "Be Your Way!" — apparently the old jingle just wasn't ME-centered enough...).

The more life centers around me, the more innately selfish and emotionally sterile I become and the more alone I truly am (even when I am surrounded by people). Loneliness gives way to selfishness and taking. That's what the Almighty alluded to just before He created Eve, with the deceptively simple declaration, "It is not good that the human be alone."[11]

Why is alone not good? If the total human is fully there, why change things?

The human as a single being was missing something absolutely vital to his humanity.

What was missing?

Giving.

As we shall see, giving — from many angles and in many forms — is the secret elixir that creates a great marriage and a great human being. This book will present the four pillars

---

11. Genesis 2:18.

that form the foundation of success in marriage. Giving is the ground upon which all four pillars stand.

WHAT'S GOOD?

We're used to thinking that being alone is "not good" simply because "It's better to have company" or "It's bad to be alone." But if the starting point was total unity and completeness, if literally nothing was missing, then surely there was no problem with being alone!

The real lack in Adam and Eve's original oneness — the "not good" of it — was that this complete being had no means for becoming truly "good." Why? Because true goodness is defined by *giving*. A single, complete, self-contained being has no reason to give. It's all there. I need nothing, and I can give nothing. In the absence of giving I have no way to get beyond my limited and selfish self.

At a still deeper level, the ultimate job of a human is to emulate the Creator. That defines my job rather differently. It's not all about me and my satisfaction. On the contrary, the real path to myself lies in making space for, giving to, and helping build the other. It seems paradoxical, but the truth is that by focusing on the other I ultimately find myself, my mission, and my happiness.

YOU-LOGY

Think for a moment. What would I like my children to say about me at my eulogy? That I was clever in business? That I was a great athlete? That no one else ever got the last word when I was around? That my taste in clothes was impeccable? That I had the most impressive car collection? The most stunning home? The best top-spin backhand? That my soufflé was the lightest? That I was better looking than my neighbors and colleagues? Really?

Most of us, when we think about it, want to be remembered as being *good* people. It may be one of the great universal truths about which few disagree. That goodness is defined by the giving we did in our lives.

"She always took care of us."

"He never let a friend down."

"She sacrificed her needs so that we could have ours met."

"He was always about the other."

"She had a smile for anyone who was feeling down."

"He cared about his community and put his money where his mouth was."

"She always fought for the downtrodden."

Despite the nearly universal agreement and clarity we have on the deeper goals of life, how much do we actually focus on those goals on a day-to-day basis?

The beauty of marriage is that it provides a constant framework of opportunity for achieving the goals that most of us hope to be remembered for. Alone, we can't give fully. If we can't give, we can't attain real goodness. There are few other truths we hold to be self-evident. How odd, then, that we spend so little time actually focusing on life's primary goal and pathway to meaning and happiness. It somehow never makes its way onto my smartphone calendar. How many of us wake up in the morning and find "giving" and "developing my goodness and greatness" on the day's agenda, along with my workout, meetings, and after-work plans? How many of us spend time focusing on how and when to give?

Marriage is about much more than curing loneliness and even more than propagating the species. That's why Adam and Eve had to be separated. They needed an opportunity to give and give and give to each other, and, in so doing, earn their oneness and completeness. That makes marriage *good*. That made each of them good. That process of giving can help make us truly good as well.

Marriage: The primary vehicle

Marriage is not just a *good* place to give and to develop our goodness. It is *the* place for life's ultimate goals to be fulfilled. If we fail to develop ourselves and our spouses in this cosmically beautiful relationship, we can't simply make up for it in other arenas. Of course, we have opportunities to give to children, friends, colleagues and the needy, as well as to our pets and our hobbies. And of course these acts of kindness and caring build ourselves and others. But the ultimate, most intense, multi-faceted, enduring, meaningful, productive, and *consistent* giving — the kind of giving that both defines us and can transform us — can best (if not *only*) be expressed through marriage.

Overcoming differences

This discovery leads to perplexing question number two: Assuming we needed to be separated to create an opportunity for giving, why did we have to be made so inscrutably *different*?! Couldn't we have each received 50% of what we were originally, right down the middle? I mean, forget about re-attaining eternal oneness — my spouse and I can hardly get through an evening without a major disagreement, let alone attain total unification!

"She's just so different from me."

"Sometimes I just don't get him at all!"

"She's impossible to please."

"He doesn't appreciate what I do for him."

"She wants me to watch a chick flick?!"

"His idea of a romantic evening is to download 'Diehard' and watch it over beer and nachos!"

"I love watching sports!"

"I hate watching sports!"

"My perfect day is shopping, lunch, and a hot cappuccino!"

"My idea of paradise is fishing in a cold river."

"Why does she insist I talk when I need time to myself?"

"Why can't he be there for me when I need him to listen?!"

"She's all business and I'm about fun."

"I need my space!"

"I need your love!"

How on earth can we be expected to come together and unify if it means crossing so many and such constant hurdles? It seems like even the best of marriages have endless ups and downs and need frequent therapy. What *was* the Almighty thinking?!

Help! I need somebody!

The very first description we have of Eve in her relationship to Adam is that she was created to be his *"ezer kenegdo."*

These Hebrew words are commonly translated as his "help meet."[12] Besides the fact that most English speakers have no idea what a "help meet" is, that translation is not accurate. A look back at the original Hebrew will help us understand the true meaning.

The original Hebrew phrase *"ezer kenegdo"* literally means "a helper (*ezer*) against him (*kenegdo*)."

What does this mean? How can she be a helper if she is against him? To understand this better, let's focus on the concept "help."

The answer reveals the deepest foundation of marriage. The job of each spouse is to help the other in every way. I help take care of her needs, and she helps take care of mine. That means we have to study each other, get to know each other, care about each other. I can't give to her if I don't know what makes her happy and I don't understand what she lacks. She can't give to me if she keeps missing me or giving me what she likes rather than what I like. We need to figure out what makes the other tick.

- I need to be left alone sometimes
- She needs to be heard
- She wants to feel appreciated and loved
- He wants to be admired
- I have to avoid things she finds upsetting or disturbing
- She needs to respect my boundaries. I need to express love to her frequently and clearly

---

12. Genesis, King James version, 2:20.

Being a true giver in marriage means getting outside of myself for the sake of my spouse. When we work to understand and properly give to each other, we create happiness and satisfaction. We also become bigger and better people in the process. That journey leads us to true oneness.

That's the "help" part of the equation. I get that. Now what is this "against" component?

Hold it against me!

Each of us enters the world as a huge bundle of needs and wants. Some have described a baby as someone who is willing to wake up half a continent because he wants a drink of water. The long and arduous process of maturation involves growing out of our natural, childish self-centeredness and into the less natural adult roles of giving and taking responsibility.

As I'm not perfect, sometimes I fail to give. I forget my real job in life. In marriage it often begins with my taking her for granted. I don't appreciate all she does for me. By taking her giving as a given, so to speak, I begin focusing more and more on *my* needs. I lose sight of hers. I make demands. All that she does becomes part of my baseline set of expectations to the point that I don't even notice the goodness in what she does for me. I do notice what she *doesn't* do for me, and I am very perceptive when it comes to her shortcomings and faults.

That's exactly when she becomes "against" me.

The feeling of confrontation, of opposition, usually begins just after the cosmic but short-lived high of romance begins to fade, sometime within a few weeks of the wedding (if we're lucky). But it is precisely at that moment that a husband or a wife has the opportunity to discover that marriage is the primary vehicle for growing as a person. That friction of "against" that gnaws at my heart when I have failed to live up to my human potential for goodness is the failsafe mechanism built into the system to remind me that I've lost my way and that it's time to refocus and start giving again.

Hew and me

The risk of this mechanism is that we may totally misread the cues. As the initial infatuation wears off and the inevitable differences and little irritants begin to appear, many spouses begin to suspect that they married the wrong person. He begins to draw away. She shuts down in response. The differences and misaligned sensitivities begin to magnify. The fighting starts. Intimacy suffers. The creeping loneliness of unhappy marriage begins to set in as each side begins contemplating escaping — if not physically, then emotionally.

The differences we discover in each other are inevitable. But lacking a proper framework for understanding what a real marriage is, we can miss the boat completely. In reality, the process of negotiating and accommodating those differences in search of a higher balance and harmony *is* the marriage. Each of us expresses needs and reactions that can appear inscrutable and maddening to each other. We don't fit so naturally together. That's by design!

When a mason comes to repair a breach in the wall, the first thing he does is take a rough stone that's *too big* for the hole. Then he carefully hews it and sands it at each point of friction, turning it round and round until at last it fits in perfectly. Without that friction the stone never gets smoothed and the wall stays broken. So it is in our marriage. The job is to take our differences and to continually grind away our rough edges until our fit is smooth. Each new stone we fit into its place in that process builds and fortifies the structure of our marriage.

Marrying someone and expecting things to just fall into place harmoniously is akin to throwing those variegated natural rough stones together and hoping they all snap into place easily and make a house.

Complement your spouse!

A mature marriage begins *not* by marrying someone who's the same as I. On the contrary, our differences are the raw notes that can become harmony. The richness of the relationship lies precisely in those areas where we function differently. Partly, it's through the growth that comes through the accommodation. Perhaps more important and more inspiring is the moment we realize that we can embrace our differences and use them to build something so much bigger and more beautiful together than we could apart.

In the business world, there are swaggering entrepreneurs, visionaries, and risk takers on the one hand, and there are conservative and careful bean-counters on the other. Most investors would be well advised to avoid either extreme when searching for the perfect investment. However, when you pair the cowboy with the buttoned up controller, something extraordinary happens. It usually begins with friction. Vision versus practical reality. Unlike in marriage, in business the value of that friction is treasured.

It's still friction, no doubt about it. But as each side realizes that it can't function without the other, the harmony begins to take shape. That's where real value is built, a shared goal pursued by harmonized but opposite perspectives, a sum greater than the parts.

In marriage it's no different. It's precisely those unique and differing perspectives, sensitivities and natures that come together to build a bigger marriage and bigger spouses. Neither side gives up who they are. Each side brings unique talent, perspective, and energy to literally every issue that arises over a lifetime of living together.

In the beginning, when I become aware of our differences, it often feels like I have to *accommodate* my spouse's desire, needs, and visions. Meaning, I see her as limited, not able to match my broader and deeper intellect and insight. But what can I do? I took on a commitment to take care of her and make her happy and work together....

As we mature in our marriage, however, I learn to get out of myself and my narrow, self-centric world (however deep and smart I may be) and slowly I lower my defensiveness. As this process occurs, I often, if not always, happily discover that the differing or opposing vision of my spouse actually complements my picture of reality, whether the issue involves how we spend our time, how we raise our kids, or simply how to relate to the opportunities and challenges that life constantly throws our way. Just as each of my eyes by itself has no depth perception until they work together to view an object, so do our combined talents and sensitivities create greater wisdom and possibilities than either of us can achieve alone.

In mystical terms, that creation of a more perfect perception, unity, and reality occurs when two spouses, often polar opposite beings, come together as one. The underlying spiritual forces that merge into a complete being are known in the ancient sources as being "male" and "female." A clear picture of those paradigms, with their differing natures, strengths, and weaknesses, can illuminate both the pitfalls and promises of marriage. Let's turn our focus to this amazing subject — the essence of what "male" and "female" are.

Biology, Emotion & Soul

THE OPPOSITE VIEW!

The Western vision of marriage has strayed far from its ancient roots, often with catastrophic results. The problem is that often our vested interests and prejudices can prevent us from seeing what is literally in front of our noses. One of the most obvious things we miss is just how different men and women are. We have come to believe that we are really just two varieties of the same thing, that our core identities don't really differ much. Yes, we've learned, he goes to the cave to solve problems while she talks them out with friends. He loves it when friends provide solid advice and solutions while she just wants to be heard. But this just boils down to differing styles, right?

Wrong. The ancient Jewish view of marriage starts with a premise that may jar the modern ear, yet is worth spending some time considering. Namely, we may not be *at all* the same. The person I'm living with may in fact be the complete opposite of what I am, and function in a totally different mode, not just biologically but emotionally and spiritually as well. That means that the work we have to do to prepare for, or to *rebuild*, our marriages starts with a willingness to undo our pre-existing assumptions and to begin re-learning the basic paradigms of who and what my spouse is. Once I do that, I can redirect my efforts toward learning how my spouse needs me to operate in order to take care of his or her needs. That's the essence of marriage.

OUT OF THE MALE (AND FEMALE) BOX

Irrespective of our views on organized religion and ritual, all but the most dyed in the wool materialists agree that there are aspects that drive us that cannot be explained physically. Our emotions. Our sensitivities. Our inner longings. The part of me that seeks and feels love, my sense of right and wrong. At the very least we *experience* these aspects of ourselves as lying beyond the purely physical layer of who we are.

Jewish mysticism teaches that the most sublime spiritual study begins, somewhat ironically, by studying the physical, which itself is a mere manifestation of spiritual forces and identities. The spiritual axiom is that the entire physical world functions the way it does in order to reveal higher spiritual truths. In fact, we have no means for sensing the spiritual other than via the physical. There simply is no periscope for peering into the spiritual dimension. If only we would look at the physical with clear and unbiased vision, we would discern far more profound insights than any biology book could generate.

Nowhere is that more important than in the physical makeup and distinctions between a man and a woman. If we really want to know how we function at the higher emotional and spiritual levels, we need to start with biology and go from there.

It's important to note from the outset that any discussion of male-ness and female-ness is fraught with political and emotional danger. However, when we examine these human aspects in a spiritual context, the terms not only shed their relationship to gender-based issues, but they no longer refer to actual gender itself. Every individual is a complex constellation of natural and nurtured traits that may have both male and female aspects to them. For example, while emotional sensitivity is considered a female characteristic, some men function with high emotional sensitivity. Conversely, some women may function in a colder, less sensitive mode that we commonly associate with men. We need to stress the point to avoid any misunderstanding: there is no assignment of *value* to either mode; neither is better than the other. They are equal. But they are *different*.

For the purpose of developing our understanding of this idea, we'll start by equating male-ness with men and female-ness with women. Once we have the paradigms clear, we can try to figure out where along the spectrum you and your spouse fit, and what to do with that knowledge.

SEPARATE AND EQUAL

It also *should* go without saying that neither male nor female is better or worse. There is no assignment of inherent value to either mode. They are simply *different*. The millions of copies of *Men are from Mars, Women are from Venus* that have been read worldwide suggest that we're still on this side of suggesting something outrageous. On the contrary, the discovery of why it is that I feel and operate the way I do, and my spouse the way he or she does, is *liberating*. Perhaps that's the deeply resonant chord that book struck within so many readers.

I might not *like* the fact that my spouse and I reflect fundamental and inherent differences, but I ignore those differences or pretend they don't exist at my own peril. When we are not relating to each other with a clear awareness of our differences, we will not be able to build the wonderful harmony of radically different parts interlocking and working together. Understanding those differences and embracing them reduces the endless tension in marriage that stems from the expectation that my spouse should respond the way *I* would respond, act the way *I* would act, want the things that *I* would want. Marriage begins its ascent to greatness when I begin to think about the needs and desires of the other, and then commit myself to trying to fulfill them.

We all descend from a spiritual essence that is an infinite unity (as we described in Chapter 1). We're brought into a fragmented world to utilize all of our talents and energies to recreate and reflect that oneness in our physical world. In the individual, that means aligning our often competing and conflicting physical, emotional, and spiritual drives into a unified set of goals. Marriage is the ultimate arena for this work. The most intense and fulfilling realization of unity that we can experience is in a proper marriage, the primary testing ground in which we have an opportunity and a mandate to break out of our isolated, limited, and lonely worlds in order to build a more complete being with our spouse. In physical terms, together we create a child; in emotional terms, together we create a relationship, the context for continued personal development.

MALE AND FEMALE: POTENTIAL AND REALIZATION

The spiritual concept of male is defined as the ability and desire to generate energy, something new, and something with endless potential. That's why a man always needs a new project. That's why that electronic gadget that seemed so amazing last year now must be replaced. That's why after he sells his startup after years of toil, he immediately starts up another company rather than enjoying the fruits of his labor. That's why men hate spending money; it is not (necessarily) because he's cheap, but because spending it on *one thing* takes away the infinite power he has to buy *anything* with the money. That's also why men have an endless desire to relate with as many women as possible, however superficially, which constantly threatens to undermine the fabric of any relationship he has committed himself to.

The spiritual concept of female, in contrast, lies not in the ability to generate a new spark, but in the ability to pick up the spark that has been struck and, before it dies, fan it into a flame and make it real. That's why she's great with details. That's why she understands what is truly going on in her daughter's life when he thinks everything is fine. That's why she thinks that having money without ever spending it is pointless. That's why she can finish and perfect a project even if someone else originated it. That's why she longs to build a deep relationship with one person.

The problem with male sparks is that they quickly burn out. That's his limitation. It's only when the spark is picked up by a woman that the potential can be built into a fire. The female limitation is that without that spark, the fire can't get lit. But once kindled, she can fan it into a flame to light up the world.

WHERE DO BABIES COME FROM?

Let's examine human anatomy. The male and female bodies function in vastly different ways. If we really want to see it most vividly, we need look no further than the creation of a child. Within that miraculous process, the man's contribution has the key male qualities we mentioned. The male seed is noted both for how tiny it is, how multitudinous, and how short-lived. The sperm cell measures about 5 microns, or about 2 ten-thousandths of an inch. It may be the tiniest cell in the body.[13] In the average sexual encounter, a healthy man releases 30-500 *million* of those cells[14] and he may produce up to 12 *trillion* in his lifetime.[15] That's about as close to infinite potential as we can conceptualize in this world. Yet those cells, even within the hospitable environment of a woman's reproductive system, survive at most for 5 days.[16] How incredibly "male" is his contribution —

---

13. Angier, Natalie. "Sleek, Fast and Focused: The Cells That Make Dad Dad." *The New York Times.* June 12, 2007, www.nytimes.com/2007/06/12/science/12angi.html.
14. Freeman, David. "Nine Things You Never Knew About Sperm." *The Huffington Post.* December 6, 2017, www.huffingtonpost.com/2013/11/20/nine-things-you-never-knew-about-sperm-photos_n_4268031.html.
15. Angie, N.
16. Trost, Landon. "How Long Do Sperm Live...." *Healthy Lifestyle*, the Mayo

massive amounts of energy and potential, but no staying power and no reality! And, of course, the moment that spark is released, the man is finished, he cannot continue. His presence is not even *necessary* from that point on.

What is the woman's contribution to this process? Needless to say, it could not be more different from the man's. A woman is born with a finite number of eggs. The egg is among the *largest* cells in the body, with a width of about 30x the sperm cell, and actually visible with the human eye![17] She ovulates just once per month, from puberty at around 10 years old until infertility sets in around 40.[18] Of the stock of eggs she's born with, only about 500 will ever have a shot at being fertilized.

I COULDN'T HAVE DONE IT WITHOUT YOU

The physiological differences between the male and female anatomy perfectly reflect their spiritual differences. Finite versus infinite. Smallest versus largest. Short-lived versus the receptacle of life. The process of the actual fertilization happens when that *one* available egg allows *just one* of those millions of sperm cells to penetrate. Within a fraction of a second, a "lock and key" mechanism changes the egg's outer membrane to prevent any other sperm cells from penetrating. The other 100 million or so sperm cells — each of which potentially could have sparked a new life — are left to die. Lit up by that spark, the egg — in a process that

---

Clinic. May 2, 2018, www.mayoclinic.org/healthy-lifestyle/getting-pregnant/expert-answers/pregnancy/faq-20058504.
17. Angie, N.
18. Silber, Sherman J. "Beating Your Biological Clock." *The Infertility Center of St. Louis,* www.infertile.com/beating-biological.

lasts nine magical months — will produce the flame of a new, real, and whole child. The conception of a child, the awesome process of the perfect complexity of the vastly different male and female reproductive anatomies wherein each one is totally useless without the other, is the perfect paradigm for what marriage is.

EMOTION 1.01

The point here is not to refresh our knowledge of biology. The point is to ponder for a moment about how those physical differences, so manifest and dramatic, might reflect themselves in emotional differences.

In the spiritual and emotional realms, a man always needs to express his energy in a multitudinal way. As soon as one conquest is reached — and it doesn't matter whether it's in business, sports or the toys men love to play with — he's immediately bored with it and is ready to go onto the next challenge. That's why the lifelong struggle, even for an emotionally healthy man who deeply loves his wife, is to fight that same dynamic when it comes to women. After all, one woman is a limitation on his powerful, natural desire to produce newness. So, by nature, the challenge for a man is to loyally put all of that energy and spark into just one place, his marital relationship. Parenthetically, the concept of the negativity of "wasted seed" is not some medieval superstition. On the contrary, it lies in the thought that any potential channeled into the wrong place, especially when it is done for no reason other than for momentary bodily pleasure, devalues and wastes that priceless potential.

She, at the other extreme, doesn't want to flip from one

thing to another, from one conquest to another, from one man to another. A woman wants to build one thing and make it as real and beautiful and deep and powerful as possible. But just as the male has his lifelong challenge of loyalty, she also has a challenge. In the desire to build that deep and amazing singular relationship, a woman may emotionally smother a man.

REAL HARMONY — PLAYING DIFFERENT NOTES

To summarize, the essence of a man is that he always has renewing and infinite energy and a childlike spirit. His danger is that he may look for new and inappropriate places to direct that energy. His challenge and goal in marriage is to put all those sparks of newness and potential loyally into one place, where it can be built into something real. In one respect, that's a child. In another, it's the marriage itself.

The essence of a woman is her natural affinity towards loyalty and maturity, toward staying with one relationship and building it and making it real. Often, she is the adult in the relationship. Her danger is that her deep desire to consolidate the relationship may actually stifle it. Her challenge is to become big enough to inspire and absorb all of her husband's energy and newness so that he doesn't need to look anywhere else.

We see this clearly in the relationship a woman has with her child, from conception to pregnancy to childbirth to raising the child to granting ever more freedom to the teenager and onward to independence and adulthood. Throughout this process, a woman is constantly giving of herself totally for the sake of the son or daughter, only to have to rip herself away at the end of each stage, which in turn gives life to the next stage of the child's development. She experiences that pain in order not to stifle the development of the child. Incredibly, the relationship and love she feels for the child she is raising continues to deepen and broaden, not *despite* the periodic tearing away but *because* of it. That same talent can be applied to her marriage, where she provides the space and love to absorb all that newness and to constantly encourage more.

In a healthy marriage, no unique element of the male or female is purposeless. Everything has its function in building the palace of marriage. And neither partner can do it without the other.

Dissolving the partnership

Let's consider some practical ramifications of these newly discovered paradigms.

First and foremost, once I realize that my spouse and I are quite different, and necessarily so, I can at last stop thinking of marriage as a partnership. Marriage is *not* a partnership! That model has brought untold misery into marriages for decades. A partnership is an arrangement in which two sides undertake to achieve a common objective, each side with certain rights and certain obligations. He has his rights and obligations; she has hers. In the world of business, the common wisdom is that 70-80% of partnerships and alliances fail. Each side tends to focus on his own rights and on the other side's responsibilities, instead of focusing on his own responsibilities and on the other side's rights.

Businessmen joke about an old fable of a chair that,

from the beginning of time, has sat empty in heaven. It's called the chair of the happy partner.

Approaching marriage like a partnership certainly doesn't bode well for success in marriage. It is likely that no single modern myth about marriage has caused more damage, misery, and resentment.

The classical Jewish view of marriage is that it has nothing to do with partnership. Why? Because my job is to think only about *my* obligations, not about my wife's. And her job is to think about *her* obligations, and not about mine.

A great rabbinical leader and wise man of the early 1900's would often speak to the bride and groom as they were being led to the wedding ceremony. He would say to them, "Be careful, my dear ones, that you always strive to give pleasure to each other, just as you feel at this moment. And know, that at the moment you begin making demands on one another, your happiness will have departed."[19]

I GAVE AT THE OFFICE (BUT I NEED TO GIVE AT HOME)

The most ironic truth of marriage is that when a selfish spouse makes demands and becomes a taker, it only pushes the husband or wife away, but the moment that he or she gives genuinely, the natural response is for the beneficiary of the goodness to give back even more than he or she has received. The "against" is naturally transformed to "helper." The spouse becomes one's greatest ally and supporter.

The road to marital happiness and perfection begins when I give. It is toward giving that we now turn our focus.

---

19. Rabbi Eliyahu E. Dessler (1892-1953), *Strive for Truth*, Essay on Loving Kindness, pp. 38-39.

Giving

PLANE TALK ABOUT LOVE

In the spring of 2000, a small group of stock analysts from JPMorgan and senior management consultants from McKinsey and Company chartered a private plane and covered the major US cities for a "roadshow" of our new joint research project on the telecom industry. Late that night, in the luxurious setting of a G4, we chatted casually about anything other than work. When the discussion turned to family, one young analyst from JPMorgan shared a bitter complaint. His marriage, he said, then about two years old, basically stunk. Why? Because his wife had stopped acting towards him the way she had when they dated and when they were newlyweds. She simply wasn't holding up her end of the partnership anymore and no longer took care of him the same way she used to. He no longer felt her love, and in return was falling out of love with her.

Thinking it over for a moment, I — the one orthodox Jew

of the group, the one who had been married the longest, and the only one with kids at the time — said to the young man, "My friend, that's because you have a totally warped picture of what marriage is and especially of what creates love." With that, the group went silent and all heads turned.

"Okay, and why is that?" the young man responded, a bit skeptically.

I explained. "There was a great rabbi[20] who pointed out that people have the concept of love exactly backwards. We go through life with the assumption that if someone will do for me, will take care of me, will give to me properly, then of course I will love them in response. But the truth of the matter is that it's exactly the opposite — *we love where we give*. Why do parents love kids more than kids love parents? Because they give more. Why do people love their dogs? Because they take care of them. Why do people love their plants? Because they tend to them. Giving causes love; taking destroys it. You have to flip your whole paradigm and start giving and giving and giving to her — and then you'll love her. Then you'll have a real marriage."

For a long moment, the group was speechless. "Whoa!" was the first word uttered by one of the airborne analysts. After a few moments, the heads began to nod in agreement to the new paradigm for marriage — new to them, that is; but coming from an old European rabbi who had garnered the wisdom from Talmudic sources *two millennia* old.

The impression this encounter made on me was powerful: namely, that much of the ancient wisdom I had spent some years studying and integrating had a universal and

---
20. Ibid.

eternal message. If only it could be translated into the language of a modern generation.

The real surprise came a few weeks later, when one day that young analyst who had decried his failing marriage approached me at work. "You won't believe what has happened," he said, positively bouncing. "I started integrating the vision you told us in the name of that rabbi, started focusing on my giving to my wife rather than my taking from her, and our marriage has literally turned around. It's just amazing!"

Lego of old preconceptions!

What exactly was the insight that turned that young analyst's life — and marriage — around?

The answer: We feel love for those to whom we give.

Let's see this concept in action.

- Why do parents love their kids more than kids love their parents?
- Why do I love my dog more than he loves me?
- Why is my kid attached more to the simple little Lego truck that she built than to a super-fancy and expensive Lego battleship that we gave her that was already assembled?
- Why do I love my plant?
- Why do childless couples often struggle financially and emotionally for years to have or adopt children?
- More odd still: Why, after all that she has done for me, do I still not really feel love for my wife?

When I give, when I invest my time or money or energy or emotion in someone or something, I put *myself* into the other. It doesn't make a difference whether that "other" is a Lego truck or a plant or a cat or a child or a spouse. I find myself there. *It* or *he* or *she* is part of *me*. Especially in marriage, I can truly find *myself* in my spouse.

This simple notion, properly integrated, can transform your life.

WHAT GIVES?

We are used to thinking that being the recipient of somebody's kindness causes me to love the one who gives to me. If only I had someone to believe in me, take care of me, support me, cook for me, do favors for me, I'd be a loving and happy spouse filled with gratitude toward my giving husband or wife.

The direction that societal thinking and technology has taken us only compounds this concept. Today, the most popular devices on the market begin with one letter: I. There's the iPhone, the iPad, the iPod. The message? It's all about me, and I can, over time and with the help of my personal technology, have literally everything my way. My diet is idiosyncratic. Our mattress (assuming we haven't yet created a two-bedroom home to accommodate our individual needs) now divides into two sections so that I can have it soft and warm while my spouse has it medium and cool (and her head gets naturally lifted when she snores so that I don't have to be disturbed). More and more my world is being tailored to the exact desire of...me.

Yet, somehow, for some reason, despite my ability to

have it all my way, well-being is at an all time low. Faltering self-esteem, depression, perceived lack of meaning and purpose, divorce — all have reached alarmingly high levels. On the one hand, our tendency toward selfishness and narcissism is being fed more and more, and yet, on the other hand, my feeling of true well-being, that life is good, fails to prevail.

VOLUNTEERING INFORMATION

While natural cravings push us to believe that having our needs met is the key to happiness, both research and life experience suggest quite the opposite. Before turning towards marital love, let's first consider what modern research has to say about the causes of happiness in general. Consider the following:

- Research by social psychologist Liz Dunn and her colleagues, published in the journal *Science*, shows that people's sense of happiness is greater when they spend relatively more money on others than on themselves. In one survey of over 600 U.S. citizens, Dunn and colleagues found that spending money on others predicted greater happiness whereas spending money on oneself did not, and this pattern was found across all income levels.[21]

---

21. McConnell, Allen R. "Giving Really Is Better Than Receiving: Does Giving To Others (vs. The Self) Promote Happiness?" *Psychology Today*. December 25, 2010, www.psychologytoday.com/intl/blog/the-social-self/201012/giving-really-is-better-receiving.

- ❦ Americans who describe themselves as "very happy" volunteer an average of 5.8 hours per month. Those who are "unhappy" volunteer just 0.6 hours.[22]

- ❦ Americans who donate more than 10 percent of their incomes experience lower depression rates. (41 percent say they rarely or never experience depression, compared with 32 percent of those who do not donate more than 10 percent.)[23]

- ❦ Americans who are very giving in relationships — being emotionally available and hospitable — are much more likely to be in excellent health (48 percent) than those who are not (31 percent).[24]

- ❦ In his book *Flourish*, Martin Seligman, founder of Positive Psychology, writes that "scientists have found that doing a kindness produces the single most reliable momentary increase in well-being of any exercise we have tested."

Why is that? It seems counterintuitive that giving away my money, time, and energy to others should give me more happiness. Surely, it should be getting what I want that does the trick!

---

22. Smith, Jordan M. "Want to Be Happy? Stop Being So Cheap!" *The New Republic*. September 22, 2014, www.newrepublic.com/article/119477/science-generosity-why-giving-makes-you-happy.
23. Smith, J. M.
24. Smith, J. M.

No middle ground

Our exploration[25] of why giving is so healthy begins with a key premise: every human is created with two fundamental and opposing desires and capabilities — giving and taking. The ability to give — to do good for the other, to have compassion, to share, to support — without taking anything in return echoes the loftiest expression of the Almighty, and forms the most beautiful and noble of human traits. It epitomizes elevated and truly *human* behavior.

Taking, at the other extreme, is defined by its desire to pull towards myself, for my own benefit, anything that enters my orbit. This is what we refer to as selfishness, and it lies at the core of everything that is ugly and destructive in life, from wars and exploitation on the world stage, to murder, theft, and trickery in the criminal realm, to destructive and abusive relationships in the personal sphere.

The most radical element of this premise, however, is that when it comes to giving and taking, *there is no middle ground*. Every act, every word, and every thought relating to anyone or anything outside of the self may be traced to a root-level desire either to give or to take.

The notion that giving is an expression of the Divine image that exists in all of us and taking is anti-Divine and anti-human helps us understand the famous words of King Solomon: "The one who hates gifts will live."[26] Real life and life affirmation are expressed through giving. Giving makes me feel so good because when I give, I am truly alive.

---

25. These ideas are based on the insights of Rabbi Eliyahu E. Dessler in "Essay on Loving Kindness," in *Strive for Truth* (volume I).
26. Proverbs 15:27.

The roots of love

Before we turn to romantic love, let's first examine the general concept of love and its relationship to giving.

If we search deeply enough, we'll uncover sparks of giving in virtually every human being, even those we consider terribly self-centered. Where do we see it? Consider how we celebrate our victories and accomplishments and major life experiences. No celebration feels complete or meaningful unless it's shared with others. No one wants to celebrate alone. This longing springs from the deepest part of the human soul. It's a spark of the desire to give.

Many people have a longing to have children. Why? Children are very expensive, demanding, and difficult; just ask any parent. The desire to have children expresses the natural human need for continuity beyond myself, for someone to carry on my name and values. But it is more than that. A person longs to find someone to give to, to love.

It's no surprise, then, to find that many people who can't have children will seek to adopt children. Still others who can't or won't have children will acquire a pet to love and care for as they would a child. This deep human quality is rooted in the desire to give that is hidden in every heart.

What causes love?

We have seen that love and giving are closely intertwined. But which one produces the other? Do we give where we love (I give to you because I love you), or do we love where we give (as a result of giving to you, I feel love for you)?

We are accustomed to thinking that giving is the outgrowth of my love. While one way of expressing love is through giving, the truth is that giving produces love. A person loves the fruit of his hard work. Why? Because where I invest my time and energy and sweat and tears, I find a piece of myself that lives in the recipient of my toil, whether it's the daughter I raised, the baby I nursed, the dog I took care of, plant I tended, or house (or Lego set, if I am a child) that I built. Every one of us feels attached to the work of our hands because we find ourselves there.

Many of us shy away from giving, fearful that we'll lose what little we have. But giving to another is actually the most effective way to build one's self. When I give to the other, far from losing what I have, I expand my self. All that I bestow creates a new part of myself within the other, making "me" greater and larger, whether within my spouse, my child, my pet, my plant, or my Lego house.

Through giving I can create a true, enduring, intimate connection with another person. The process of giving that leads to closeness and oneness is what we call, and how we create, love.

A Wilde thought

Before moving on, let's elaborate on this notion of finding myself in the other. We'll start with an axiom: The most enduring and consistent love, the love that knows no betrayal, the love that virtually every human being will experience in life is...self love. Think about it. If my mother doesn't feel well, I'll take her to the doctor. If that doesn't solve the problem, I'll help her find another doctor and take her there as well. And so on, to a third and a fourth doctor. But at a certain point, when I get that call from her while I'm at work, I'll hesitate before answering. At some point it becomes somewhat burdensome, if not irritating, and I'll start thinking of ways to share or pass on the responsibility. To be sure, I'll have more staying power with Mom than with Uncle Fred, and I'll stick with Uncle Fred longer than I will with my friend or acquaintance. Of course, with a spouse or child my commitment will be stronger still.

Yet how many of us *ever* have the feeling that we're too irritated, busy, or burdened to get *ourselves* to another doctor? When it comes to my own health and well-being (or career or investments or vacations), I'll search endlessly without giving it a second thought. It may be a bit hard to swallow, but there are literally no lengths to which we would not travel to secure our own happiness and well-being. As Oscar Wilde once quipped: "To love oneself is the beginning of a lifelong romance."

This idea is illustrated by a well-known story, cute but profound. The Kotzker Rebbe, a well-known Jewish leader from the European city of Kotzk, once asked a student why he was eating fish. The student replied, "Because I love fish!" The great rabbi responded, "Because you love fish, that's why you trapped the fish, pulled it out of the water, killed it, cooked it, and ate it? If you loved fish, you'd have left it swimming happily in the sea. The reason you are eating fish is because you love yourself!"

Unfortunately, for many of us, love starts with self-love and ends with self-love, and we never get past the accompanying selfishness. Anecdotally and experientially, we realize that many of the most negative and unhappy people who walk this earth are those who have been spoiled, to whom too much has been given, and who can't break the cycle of taking. Success and happiness lie in the utilization of self-love as a means of expanding into love and concern for the other.

I NOW PRONOUNCE YOU...

With this new vision of where love comes from, we turn to our goal of understanding the love between husband and wife. From where comes the powerful emotion for another human being? Is it an instinct planted within us in order to ensure the propagation of the species, much as the feeling of hunger is the instinct that reminds us to eat to keep ourselves alive? Surely, plain old and simple sexual desire would suffice for that. Why does love need to be added to the mix?

Some claim that love of the spouse is a product of gratitude, the thanks we feel and give to each other in return for fulfilling each other's needs and desires. While gratitude is essential for any healthy relationship (as we will discuss in Part II), gratitude is not love. A child loves her doll or Lego house, an adult loves the sculpture he crafted, but there is no gratitude towards that object. We'll have to keep searching for the definition of love.

COMPLETING THE PICTURE

The deeper love, beyond mere sexual attraction, that husbands and wives feel for each other arises as each completes the other. As we said in Chapter 1, each of us enters this world as half a human. Through giving to and bonding with my spouse, we become a single, unified image, both physically and spiritually. As we work to complete each other, our love develops. We love where we give. And no arena is more filled with the full spectrum of opportunities to give as a marriage. Helping, listening, supporting, encouraging, providing, sharing. All of these manifold activities help to complete each other and to create love.

Short shelf life

Let us now ask the disturbing question that haunts us all: Why is it that most of the time, love doesn't last?

There is a simple, but extraordinary, answer to this question. As we noted at the start of this section, the human being is created with two fundamental and mutually exclusive powers: giving and taking. For a period of time, awakened to the intoxication and promise and salvation of romantic love, we rise to the level of givers. That giving produces love. Anyone who has tasted it understands that it is the Almighty's greatest gift to humankind. The cascading effect of feeling whole and loved and loving and quintessentially human transforms the lives of husband and wife.

But as time passes, often very little time at that, the lower natural tendency towards taking reasserts itself. An emotional reversion to the mean. Some of us can even pinpoint the moment it happens. One day we awaken to realize that in place of the giving and loving that created our powerful oneness and completion, we have sunk down to our lower state as takers.

It's easy to spot. In place of seeking to make the other happy and fulfilled, we find ourselves making, or being subjected to, demands. You owe me. You're not fulfilling your end of the deal. I want you to.... And so begins the death spiral of romantic love and oneness. So simple, so tragic. We mentioned earlier the advice that a great rabbi used to give to the young couple on their way to their marriage ceremony. "Be careful, my dear ones," he would say, "that you always strive to give pleasure to each other, just as you feel at this moment. And know, that at the moment you begin making demands on one another, your happiness will have departed."

THE PAUSE THAT REFRESHES

At first glance, the insight that love is the outgrowth of giving can give us pause. I mean, who can live up to that? Aren't we really all takers by nature (if "nature" means the way we act when we stop proactively working to make ourselves human)? That's a pretty scary thought.

There are, however, two powerful positives that arise from this knowledge and understanding. Both consist of shattering the two myths that ironically crush our ability to experience real and lasting love.

MYTH #1: MARRIAGE IS ROMANCE

Let's once and for all put to rest the myth that romance — the intoxicating, take-my-breath-away, otherworldly feeling — is love. It's not love. Romance is the short-lived inspirational period that we experience as a gift at the beginning of a relationship to get the ball rolling. Through romance we can experience, if temporarily, the powerful desire to give, to make happy, to provide, to care for. For a moment we're lifted above our natural, taking self and given a vision of what we can truly be *if I can spend the rest of my life focusing on giving to my spouse*. That short-lived period is given for free; it hasn't been worked for or earned. And like most freebies, it has a very short shelf-life. Don't expect it to last and don't confuse it with real love.

Myth #2: Great marriages just happen

Clarity on what causes love leads to the realization that the promise and happiness of marriage is squarely in your hands, not in those of your spouse. It doesn't depend on luck or karma, it isn't written in the stars. The marriage mantra you'll hear from us, and will need to repeat over and over to yourself is: It all depends on me.

There it is. We've said it. It's in my hands. In Part II of this book we'll address practical steps you can take that flow from these big conceptual insights. But don't wait for Part II. Grab a few notecards right now and write down on each one the words, "My marriage and my happiness depend solely on me." Place one in your sock drawer so you see it when you wake up. Put one in your desk drawer at work so you will see it during your busy day. Type the words into your smartphone calendar so that you can remind yourself on your way home.

Giving, as we'll see in Part II, takes on many forms, both large and small. How well I listen to my spouse and empathize with her challenges and problems, how I take care of the other's physical needs and desires, how I surprise and spoil the other, how I share myself — no list of the details can complete the picture. However, there are three underlying principles that must form the core of my giving.

To whom it may concern

First, I have to make my spouse the center of my concern in life. Nothing is more destructive to my spouse's sense of well-being than the suspicion (or knowledge) that she comes second in my life. Who competes for my attention? My job. My investments. My hobbies. Social media.

While no one would admit that any of these areas of activity, however important, take precedence over my spouse, how clearly do we actually show that in our behavior? How many times, in the middle of dinner or a date night, do I pull out my smartphone, all but removing myself from the moment I was sharing with my beloved? How many important events have been forgotten or missed due to my preoccupation with work? Yes, I'll do my best to sit and listen to her as she describes her difficult day, but is it with the same rapt attention she sees that I give my buddy when he's telling me about his latest exploits?

Deep down many spouses, especially wives, fear they are not being carried in the forefront of their partner's mind. They may take up space on the hard drive, but they're just not in the RAM. That's where the next project, the golf game, the unwritten email seems to take precedence.

The very air we breathe in marriage consists of the security we enjoy by being at the center of my spouse's life and concern and love, and that there is no real competition.

Building the other

The **second** towering idea is that the ultimate aim of giving, and my chief responsibility, is to focus on building the other. Almost any encounter with my spouse is an opportunity to build her up or tear her down. We're not just referring to praise (which must be plentiful, and can almost never be too much) versus criticism (which must be minimized and only, if ever, delivered in the right way at the right time, as we'll discuss in Part II). At a deeper level, this means empowering my spouse, showing him that I look up to him as a leader and great person, making clear to her that I trust her judgement and decision-making. I have the power to help build my spouse into bigger and better versions of herself, or to reduce her.

Affirmation, empowerment, expressions of trust, listening with interest, helping to restore or create confidence in areas outside the comfort zone, helping to succeed — all of these create a positive and achievable expectation of a bigger role that my spouse can and will step into as a more confident, competent and happy person. Criticizing, shutting down rather than engaging, controlling behavior and belittling will produce a reduced, less competent, insecure, and unhappy person.

We get it in the world of career. Any great manager gets the best out of his or her people. Weak and insecure leaders get what they want via bullying and threats, but that implodes over the longer term as toxic environments ultimately destroy the work along with the employees (and boss). Real success lies in building confidence and competence and fostering creativity and higher and higher goals. No one has ever been criticized to greatness.

We see it so clearly in our business life. The trick is to focus on building similar growth and confidence in my spouse.

Rags and riches

The Governor of New Jersey was once driving with his wife and pulled into a gas station. The attendant said hello to the Governor's wife, calling her by her first name. Sensing her husband's surprise, his wife explained that she had actually dated that guy in college, a few years before meeting the future leader of the state. "Well," he quipped, "I guess you did a bit better winding up with a Governor rather than a gas station attendant!"

"No," his wife replied with nonchalance, "had I married him, he'd have become Governor."

The old Jewish adage holds that a woman can turn a king into an old rag, or an old rag into a king. And so it is with our ability to lift up or tear down our spouse.

Dates from the palm

The **third** key driver of marital happiness lies in intimacy. Sexuality on its own, stripped of love and commitment, has been around forever (or at least as long as teenage males have walked the planet). But in recent years a potent combination of factors has begun to glorify casual sex as an *ideal*, rather than as a cheap substitute.

- TV and movie comedies and dramas routinely depict heros and heroines in pursuit of ever more frequent or daring sexual experiences — slowing and subtly changing our *view* of sex without love and commitment.

- ❦ Dating apps dedicated to maximizing "hook-up" opportunities have increased the *ease of finding* sexual partners. No longer even a need to prowl around bars and clubs all night.
- ❦ The ubiquity of smartphones has driven pornography freely and frequently into the hands of our entire society, including children. Once upon a time a teenage boy had to walk into a convenience store, terrified of being caught, and pretend he was 18 if he wanted to buy a dirty magazine (much of which would qualify as tame in the internet age). Now he just reaches into his pocket and they are in the palm of his hand. And the content is free and unfiltered.

Consistent with other trends in our selfie-centric society, sexuality is an ever-more paved pathway to the relief, pleasure, and power that we crave. It's all about how *I* feel and what *I* want at any given moment.

Do I "know" my spouse?

The role that sexuality plays in marriage is far more profound. Intimacy completes the circle — along with spiritual and emotional connection — of the total connectivity and oneness to which marriage aspires. Indeed, the physical component may be the most important driver of that connectivity, the act that lights up the entire set of circuits, body and soul.

In the Bible, the first described act of physical intimacy uses a language of "knowledge": "And Adam knew his wife Eve."[27] We're used to giggling when we hear this verse. It's

27. Genesis 4:1.

sort of the cute and embarrassed way the Almighty refers to the sexual act. Of course, this is not the intent behind the words, and perhaps no critical idea has become less understood throughout history.

It's very easy to say that two animals had relations; the male and female animals come together to mate. The idea expressed in Genesis is that the act of relations between Adam and Eve was not an animalistic act of mating. It was an act that took them to a sublime and transcendent place. A place of full knowledge of each other. We can know a friend intimately, but that knowledge has a limit. The full sharing of self, beyond intellect and emotion, comes uniquely in the physical bonding between husband and wife. That is intimacy. That's where our longing to become one with the other, to experience the echo of the cosmic oneness of the original human, is met.

Far from the cheapened version of sexuality we've been sold all our lives, the true reward of intimacy in marriage, ironically, is found in *giving* pleasure to my spouse. Anyone can imitate the sensory stimulation that is also experienced by the rest of the animal world. But sexual intimacy that grows to a crescendo from our love, care, and commitment, exists in another dimension of satisfaction.

No surprise is it, then, to discover that married couples, even as they age, have more satisfying and more frequent sex than do couples who merely live together or who simply hook up.[28]

---

28. Findings from the National Survey of Sexual Health and Behavior (NSSHB), Center for Sexual Health Promotion, Indiana University. *Journal of Sexual Medicine*, vol. 7, supplement 5.

Lack of intimacy tends to harm both husbands and wives, with risks to a couple's feelings of happiness and security in the relationship. Sexual frustration can drive a man to levels of physical and emotional discomfort that wind up, over time, finding release in many unhealthy areas, such as pornography or extra-marital affairs. For a woman, lack of intimacy may even be linked biologically to increased risk of depression.[29]

Unfortunately, in our too-busy, highly distracted and stressed-out lives, we may fail to make the effort to take care of our spouses sexually. Giving, applied to this area, means making available the time and space in my heart (and in my schedule) to take care of my spouse's needs. Partly it's a matter of frequency. And partly it's a matter of focus and sensitivity to my partner's preferences and pace.

When intimacy works, many other problems and irritants in life sort of disappear, or at least we perceive them as, well, less irritating. Sexuality, when it comes along with love and care and commitment, provides a pleasure and sense of well-being that goes beyond the temporary physical high. As is true in most realms of giving, when I focus on making the other happy, I wind up the greatest beneficiary and experience far greater pleasure myself. Such is the paradoxical but true virtuous cycle of giving.

In Part II of this book, we'll discuss strategies to help bring and sustain positive growth in these key generators of marital well-being.

---

29. Gallup, Gordon G. Jr., et al. "Does Semen Have Antidepressant Properties?" *Archives of Sexual Behavior*. June, 2002, doi.org/10.1023/A:1015257004839.

DELIVERING THE GOODS

The idea that I myself have the power to create and sustain a great marriage may be the most empowering idea that exists in the world of love.

Marriage provides life's most fundamental vehicle for continual and broad-based giving. The intoxication of romance and attractions get the ball rolling. But it quickly gives way to the life-long journey of building a real relationship, one based in giving and giving some more.

Where you give, you love. The more you give, the more you love. The more you love, the more you will tend to receive love back and the more you will expand yourself and find yourself and feel your own goodness and greatness. The more you create and experience real love through giving, the more good you create. And the more good you become. That goodness drives happiness.

While we're on the subject, let's shatter another myth. Happiness is not a goal. It's a consequence. The outcome of expanding and completing myself and my spouse will naturally produce a feeling of well-being. Not trivial pleasure, but a real feeling that life is good, that the more I give, the more I love and am loved. That the more I invest in and build my spouse, the bigger I become. A life of comfort rarely leads to happiness. But a life of growth and meaning and love cannot but lead to happiness. That happiness, generated in a healthy marriage, provides the ultimate fuel for continued giving and growth in life's ultimate virtuous cycle.

It's in your own hands.

Make it (like) work

You *can* make a great marriage, but the key word is *make*. Giving takes work. And more work. Pretty daunting.

Here's our advice: Try to take your marriage as seriously as you do your job. When it comes to my job and career I seldom lose my cool, I *always* look my best, I take great care in my speech, I continually train and push for better performance, I'm subject to periodic reviews, I aim endlessly to please my boss and clients and colleagues. Late night? Early mornings? No problem. I literally will do *anything* not to fail, and I'm ever sensitive to the expectations others have of me.

We hardly ever question the endless demands that our careers place upon us. And that's just our careers. Nearly all of us believe, or at least espouse, that our families are more important than our jobs.

The key to a great marriage is to begin to apply the same set of expectations of ourselves that we do in our jobs to our marriages. Excellence, sensitivity, always being there. If we would take our marriages even a fraction as seriously as we take our careers, we would — and can — create the relationships of our dreams and make them the center of our happiness.

Creative destruction

Despite a growing societal acceptance of the idea that marriage is not a necessity in this day and age, we have nonetheless witnessed an explosion of interest in the subject, particularly on the topic of how to save it. Indeed, the focus on marriage in the popular media has never been higher. Google "how to help marriage" and you'll receive no fewer than 255,000,000 results. Huffington Post has a "marriage advice" section on its website replete with, well, advice. While it does not yet have a marital advice section, even the venerable *New York Times* (the *New York Times*!) has been publishing about 3 articles per week on how to save or fix or upgrade your marriage!

Unfortunately, rather than reflecting clarity and understanding of the subject matter, such a cacophony of views and tricks and strategies suggests a certain desperation to find something, *anything*, that will help us find, develop and preserve our marriages — at least in name if not in structure. The reason we raise this issue here? Because rather than focusing couples on the core issue of giving, these new strategies more often than not head in *exactly* the opposite direction, playing on our most selfish instincts. Make it more about me and all will be fine.

Ironically and sadly, however, the more "creative" the ideas become, the further we stray from the old fashioned definition and structure of marriage and from its roots in giving and focusing on the other, the more elusive does that love and happiness become.

We'll mention just two....

OPEN AND SHUT

In their zeal to save some semblance of marriage, growing numbers of couples and therapists have begun to devise new marital strategies that paradoxically threaten to upend marriage itself. In particular, growing anecdotal evidence suggests that many unhappy, or unfulfilled, couples have begun experimenting with what they call "open marriage." Some refer to it as *"ethical* adultery," in which spouses take on additional lovers to make up for the needs that are not, or are no longer, being met by the spouse. All is done with the blessing and knowledge of the spouse, and hence it's not cheating and is thus "ethical." On the contrary, it is often described as salvation for the struggling marriage. I love my wife, but she just isn't attractive to me anymore. She gained too much weight. I love my husband and would never leave him, but since he became ill he can no longer satisfy my physical needs, if indeed he ever could. She never made the money she promised she would. He has lost his charm with age. I was 23 when I committed my life to you, but now I'm 35 and things have changed. How can a decision made at 23 be expected to have permanent consequences? Divorce? No way! We're committed to each other. We want to remain there for the kids or for financial reasons or because we are still such close friends. No one gets hurt, so what could be wrong?

The notion of the "open marriage" is viewed by some as a justifiable means to the noble goal of saving a marriage. Just by sort of stretching the definition of "marriage" to include others in the picture, a couple may believe that a dying marriage can be resuscitated. The problem is that at the very moment that the boundaries of monogamous intimacy are breached, the marriage is no longer a marriage in any sense other than legal. We define marriage much as our grandparents did: a unique relationship founded on an absolute and unending commitment and devotion of one spouse to the other. There is one person in this world to whom I totally devote myself, and there is one person in this world who is totally devoted to me. I embrace you now, and I will embrace you as we change and age. Once my heart, my happiness, my intimacy, and my most meaningful life experiences are shared with others, once we let someone else in — for all that we hope that it will allow us to stay together — we are forever ripped apart. It's no longer about us. It's about me. My spouse remains very important to me. But very important, no matter how important, is not life itself. At precisely that moment that we let someone else in, we are adrift in the world, cut off from the unique and private and intimate connection of total devotion and unity that marriage is.

It's a logical next step, in a way, from a social media vision of relationships. Nowadays, everyone is my friend; we share everything. But what happens to the true definition of friend in the process? The old fashioned definition went something like this: I have many acquaintances with whom I work and interact; I draw a slightly tighter circle of friends, with whom I can share more of myself. I then tighten the circle again to include those few people with whom I can truly share of myself; we have a bond and loyalty, and a certain level of intimacy. True intimacy, across the spectrum of physical, emotional, and spiritual, is saved for my spouse.

Social media has bent over backwards to stretch the definition of "friend" to include an ever wider circle of people. But don't be fooled. Anyone who has 100 best friends has *no* friends, certainly not in a meaningful sense. In that context, the chance for creating and preserving real intimacy dwindles.

Rather than argue about what technically qualifies as a

marriage, then, we'll simply define our terms as two people committed to building a private, intimate, intense, and totally devoted and loyal relationship with his or her spouse. While we may spend most of our day apart in our separate careers and hobbies, our relationship and my spouse's well-being and happiness will forever form the center of my concern. I am there for her; she is there for me — physically, emotionally, and spiritually. Even as we retain our unique identities and interests, we together form a oneness that transcends both of us.

A spouse and a half equals no real spouse, and no marriage, since it revolves around *me* and not around *us*. As to "open marriage," let's at least agree to call it by another name, however ethical some claim it to be.

SEPARATE BUT EQUAL

Another idea on the rise for saving marriage, especially amongst the wealthy: separate master bedrooms. Real estate media reports of a budding trend appeared as early as 2007[30] and as we write the quest for separate master bedrooms continues to grow, particularly at the higher end of the market. According to a survey of builders and home shoppers, about a third of purchasers seeking homes of the $1million+ price range expressed interest in the option.[31] Another survey reported that at the $2million+ price range,

---

30. Rosenblum, Gail. "Suite Idea: Dual Master Bedrooms." *Star Tribune*. April 13, 2015, www.startribune.com/suite-idea-dual-master-bedrooms/299360941.
31. Gamerman, Amy. "The Secret to a Happy Marriage? Two Master Bedrooms." *The Wall Street Journal*. March 16, 2017, www.wsj.com/articles/the-secret-to-a-happy-marriage-two-master-bedrooms-1489672201.

the percent seeking dual masters climbs to two thirds![32] Reasons cited? It's the new *"secret to happy marriage."* We don't have the same sleep schedules. I binge on Netflix while he goes to bed early. She snores. He tosses and turns in his sleep. She gets up early to exercise while he likes to sleep in. Besides, we can always snuggle up in his room when we feel affectionate — and then retreat when the mood passes.

The trend hardly surprises us. Just another symptom of the "have it your way" syndrome. No need to adjust to my spouse's needs and quirks and idiosyncrasies. Why *should* I?

We're not unsympathetic to couples facing serious sleeping disorders. But it's far from clear that two thirds of well-heeled buyers suffer from serious sleep issues. To the contrary, we've been more and more trained to have everything just as we like it with fully customized experiences. It starts with how we like our online news. It ends in the bedroom. But much as the separate vacation idea mentioned later in Part Two is likely over time to create distance when the goal is closeness, so too separate bedrooms will create better sleep — but less commitment, self-control, tolerance and giving — the key components of a real marriage.

---

32. Brophy, Beth. "Boomers Drive Hot New Housing Trend." *AARP.* March 27, 2017, www.aarp.org/home-family/your-home/info-2017/boomers-drive-housing-trend-fd.html.

PART TWO

The Four Pillars of Giving

Overview of the Four Pillars

AS WE ESTABLISHED in Part One of this book, giving creates the air and energy required for a marriage to flourish. Marriage in turn provides the greatest and most extensive set of possibilities in which giving can be activated. A virtual platform for loving kindness. Couples who enter into marriage (and remain there!) with a mindset directed toward giving can ride that virtuous cycle to the Eden of happiness, security, and oneness even amidst a life filled with stresses and challenges.

Yet telling a young (or old) husband or wife simply to "be a giver" can overwhelm even the best-intentioned among us. Too broad. Too vague. Not user friendly! With that in mind, we can turn to Part Two, in which we have categorized the infinitely rich concept of giving into four primary arenas. We refer to them as the four pillars of giving in marriage. They provide a practical framework within which we can direct and focus our actions.

None of the four pillars truly exists without the other three; all spill over into each other in a powerful, positive fashion. Nor is it possible to focus on one to the exclusion of the others; you can't make marriage fresh while remaining disrespectful, or work on gratitude while remaining under the illusion that it depends on your spouse to change the dynamic.

But as Laozi said, a journey of a thousand miles begins with a single step — and so too the work of giving in marriage. Thus, we'll break the work into the four pillars, each of which features an overview of understanding, followed by several practical steps.

The four pillars are:

1. Keep it fresh
2. Gratitude: feel it and show it
3. Respect in all its forms
4. Responsibility: it all depends on me!

A word on how to stand up the pillars

The four major arenas for giving in marriage are themselves comprised of numerous concepts and details. In order to make the process of integration user friendly, we suggest the following:

- ❦ Read all four sections to get an overview. Do it together or separately, but discuss the framework frequently with your spouse. As you go through the sections, make date nights to discuss them. What rings with you? What do you disagree with? Where do you feel you can reap the most immediate benefits?
- ❦ Decide together on one section that you'd like to work on. Give yourselves at least a month, and focus your efforts there. Again, use date nights to discuss it and encourage each other, and to praise your spouse for the benefits that have accrued to you through his

efforts. Let her know how you felt when she tried to show you respect or gratitude. Stay put on that section as long as you feel it is bearing fruit! Then move on to the next.

- Although it may seem counterintuitive, begin with a section that deals with an area in which you already are succeeding to some degree. That's called working from your strengths, and it will create positive momentum for a great beginning.
- Work on the same thing at the same time!
- Whenever you are working on something, make sure that two fundamentals remain in your focus, as they will feed each other in a virtuous cycle.
- *ACTIONS:* Choose some of the concrete suggestions and just do them! When it comes to giving, repetition is your best friend (next to your spouse) as it will create not only great habits, but a new inner reality.
- *THOUGHTS:* Read the section you're working on, then read it again after you've begun the work, and again and again. Each time you'll pick up on more nuances and gain new insights.

STATING THE OBVIOUS

All four pillars share a common axiom: my job in marriage is to function in the way that my spouse needs. It isn't about what I can get, but what I can give. As Gary Chapman so eloquently laid out in *The Five Love Languages,* and as we have seen over and over in our work with couples, it isn't enough to give. Rather, giving must be packaged in a form that your spouse can and wants and needs to receive. When I give the way *I* wish to receive, rather than the way *she* does, the giving can go unnoticed and her deeper needs unmet. This can produce ironic, but lethal, results. I may feel, quite justifiably, that I'm constantly doing for her, and that it nearly always goes unappreciated. At the same time, despite my efforts, she may be left feeling like I don't care about her and don't expend much energy on her real needs.

In order to function properly, and in order to give in a form that my spouse can receive, I first have to figure out just who my spouse actually is; otherwise, I may keep missing the mark even if I really try to be a giver and a lover.

GET OUT OF YOURSELF

Who is my spouse, exactly? What makes her tick? Which emotional and physical needs does she specifically need me to fulfill? To be sure, not all needs and desires can or have to be addressed by the spouse. If she loves to play tennis, and he either hates it or is inept at it, then let her play with a friend or trainer. If he loves to talk politics and it bores her to tears, let him determine the best economic policy of some distant land (as most men feel is part of their male civic duty) with a so-inclined buddy.

But some needs — intimacy, perhaps financial support — can *only* be taken care of by the spouse. In between lie such needs as appreciation and love, which may well get divided among many constituents in the life of each of us. I may find appreciation at work. I may well be the lucky recipient of love from my parents or relatives or friends. But few spouses can feel sufficiently, let alone wholly, appreciated or loved if the spouse can't or won't provide appreciation and love.

The only way to start the process is by getting out of yourself. We'll say it from a male perspective, but it's equally true from hers: I have to *learn* her, to sense her. Her aspirations and dreams, her fears and insecurities. Otherwise, I risk hitting a bullseye on the wrong target.

So start talking to her. Show, and make sure you have, real interest. Ask her questions about the things she likes and loves and fears and dislikes and hates. Oh yes, and *try to listen* to the answers. Pay attention to all the non-verbal clues and reactions. And then try to act upon it. Make it real. You'll be surprised by how much deeper and more fascinating and alluring she is than you ever imagined. There's only one way to plumb those depths: begin the exploration.

It's hard to overstate the complexity of the drama playing out in every marriage.

Now, let's get started with the real work!

PILLAR #1:
Keep it Fresh!

SHORT SHELF LIFE

Human beings love new things — projects, foods, vacation destinations, gadgets. We thrive on newness and freshness. Even challenges are anticipated with a certain eagerness, whether a new job, a new position in the old company, the start of the new school year, with its rush of excitement and anticipation for what the future holds. Every new thing and experience is a chance to exit the doldrums and boredom of our lives and to clean the slate.

Nowhere is this more crucial, and more neglected, than in our marriages. All new relationships begin with an explosion of energy and optimism. As the Beatles put it in 1964: "There is one thing I'm sure of — I will love her forever."[33]

---

33. From "Every Little Thing" (*Beatles for Sale*, 1964), by J. Lennon and P. McCartney.

As quaint and perhaps dated as that sounds, we all feel that way at the beginning of a love affair. But as we experience time and again, the intoxication and romance phase withers, usually much faster than we'd ever imagined (and one thing we're pretty sure of is that he didn't love her forever, maybe not even until "Help...").

THE STARLET PARADOX

Many men in particular feel that if only their wife looked like [fill-in-the-blank with today's current Hollywood starlet], especially if she could cook like his mother, he'd be romantically intoxicated forever. Yet the still-thriving world of tell-all magazines at the checkout line relies on the assumption that about every other year the handsome actor tires of his former heartthrob wife, cheats on her, undergoes public flogging and then moves onto the next starlet. Now why exactly does that happen, especially since she is often still just as gorgeous as the day he cheated with her on his prior former-model wife?

Nor is the (now-coined) "starlet paradox" limited to screen idols (or to men — women also suffer from the malady). In 2003, American and European researchers tracked 1,761 people who got married and stayed married over the course of 15 years. The findings — confirmed by more recent research — were clear: Newlyweds enjoy a big happiness boost that lasts, on average, just two years. Then the special joy wears off and they are back to where they started, at least in terms of happiness.[34]

---

34. Lyubomirsky, Sonja. "New Love: A Short Shelf Life." *The New York Times*. December 1, 2012, www.nytimes.com/2012/12/02/opinion/sunday/new-love-a-short-shelf-life.html.

In short, no matter who and how dazzlingly attractive the spouse is, the romance doesn't last. So, again, the question is: Why not? Where did it go? Why does it end so quickly? Why did fate (or the Almighty) trick us with that amazing but short-lived feeling of optimism and aliveness? Were we duped? Is it a cruel cosmic joke? Is there anything we can do to restore it?

When my smartphone — which seemed so dazzling and shiny and fast only two years ago — no longer excites me, that's the moment I decide to upgrade. In the home, we re-model (what were we thinking when we bought that sofa?). In vacations, we try London this time instead of Paris. But what about marriage? There, we simply feel trapped. The major decisions and challenges, especially for the "male" (as we described in Part One), begin to revolve around how to get that freshness and newness back. With no clear pathway to restoring romance with my spouse, the alternatives begin cropping up in our heads. Cheat? Divorce and start playing the field again? Get ever more outlandish with my spouse? Resolve myself nobly to a life of drudgery, boredom, and sameness?

Must have misplaced it

The answer to these questions can determine the fate of your marriage. Freshness in marriage not only serves to generate more passion, interest, and intimacy, it also creates a powerful spillover effect of love, security, optimism, and well-being that propels happiness, and the relationship, ever higher. It is yet another context in which giving is the secret sauce.

Before we attempt to show you the game-changing strategies on how to keep your seal of freshness intact, let's examine what causes marriage to go stale in the first place. As they say, before the doctor suggests a cure, she has to first determine the malady and, if possible, how it was acquired in the first place. Part of the challenge is designed into the system of life and love itself — Divine if you will — while part has been created, nurtured, and accelerated by humankind itself.

BY DESIGN: STAGE ONE AND STAGE TWO

One of the foundational ideas in Jewish philosophy and mysticism is that reality is always created and lived out in two separate stages. The first stage is powerful, inspiring, unlimited, but very short lived. As stage one dies out, it's replaced with stage two, which is nearly its opposite: down to earth, less exciting, yet lasting, and is in fact where "real life" is lived and meaningful goals can be realized. This pattern plays out nearly everywhere in life, and it's by design. On the one hand, it creates a challenge of constantly maturing, committing, and giving. On the other hand, it ultimately provides a person with the most profound pleasure, satisfaction, and meaning that life has to offer.

Let's take our first example from human existence itself. While every human life holds many sub-stages (infant, toddler, child, teen, young adult, middle age, etc.), there are nonetheless two fundamental platforms upon which life rests: childhood and adulthood. They differ remarkably. Childhood means endless possibility: one day a pirate or ballerina, the next a doctor or detective, the next a sports star or movie star. Always busy, and — if left unabused — always happy. But as we know, childhood gives way to adulthood, and with it, limitations, work, responsibility, disappointments.

Before we lament adulthood, let's pay homage to its primary advantage. Unlike a child, who holds the infinite possibility of being *anything*, but is in fact really *nothing*, the adult can at least become *something*. Limited, workaday, not often exciting, yet it's real. Childhood is a short-lived magical time that inspires us with possibilities and big dreams so that we can then actually make something of our lives in the far longer adult stage. It is no accident as well that true meaning, purpose — and the happiness that ensues as a consequence — belong strictly to those who accomplish within the world of stage two. Woe to that adult (usually a man) who remains emotionally in the child stage, unable to commit to becoming something real for fear of missing out on all the other possibilities — that's the guy who can't marry, can't stick with a single profession, can't spend money, just can't commit.

OUTER SPACE AND DOWN TO EARTH

Now let's take a more pointed example of this pattern: romance and love. As we know, romance is that cosmic, euphoric state that gets us involved. No matter our expectations, and Beatles aside, it doesn't last. Romance is a pure "stage-one" experience. Love forms stage two of the relationship. More down to earth than cosmic, more sober than intoxicating. Yet it is real, and it at least has a *possibility* of lasting. Success in this stage drives the true and lasting pleasure we all crave in marriage.

Just as a great childhood can lead to a meaningful and productive adulthood, so too can (and should, assuming it was not solely physically-based) romance lead us to love. The stage-one experience gets us involved — whether with visions of our personal possibilities or in the context of a relationship with another — and inspires us to make a commitment. It gets us into the game. Without it we'd be hopelessly unambitious and perpetually alone. But by design, stage one doesn't last longer than it takes to set the hook for stage two, which is where real lives and real relationships are built.

The classic mistake we make is when we assume, especially in the world of relationships, that stage one is, and should last, forever. Tragically, many of us never learn from that erroneous view of reality which has been beaten into us by an endless set of images from movies, songs, and stories. We seek that high, over and over again, only to find recurrent disappointments. Romance fades. I guess he was the wrong one. The next one will last forever. Same strategy. Same failure, over and over again. Just where exactly is that vaunted human capability to learn from mistakes?

The mature person uses that inspirational stage as a prelude to real commitment. And that's exactly the point at which a real relationship of giving and loving can truly get under way.

The takeaway? It's no accident; it's by design.

Mad men indeed

As if the nature of life and love itself had failed to create sufficient challenge to marital freshness, the combination of advertising and social media have conspired to sabotage us still further.

Global spending on advertising in 2015 reached something in the neighborhood of half a *trillion* dollars. In the US alone, companies spend more than $800 a year on every single adult. Why? Clearly some portion goes to persuading us that theirs is better than the competitor's. But largely, advertising is there to *create* a sense of need, desire, and urgency. Thought you were okay with what you had? Think again! You *need* something newer, better, faster, cooler. What you have already is out of date, no longer up to the image that they have created for you to aspire to. Just ask yourself — that wide tie in your closet, the one with the paisleys, that you are humiliated to show your friends. Exactly what were you thinking at the time of purchase? That it was new! Cool! And why was that? Because someone made you feel that that narrower blue number with the subtle stripes was *pathetic* and stale. Let's not even speak about the world of technology, where products are designed with a *built-in* obsolescence cycle. That means you buy it *expecting* to tire of it and trade up within two to three years.

Simply put, we have become a society that has been conditioned — even beyond our natural need — to outgrow, throw away, and replace nearly everything in our physical lives. Beyond any natural craving, we have conditioned ourselves to *crave* freshness.

Antisocial Media

More pernicious still, social media is slowly robbing us of our ability to appreciate and enjoy our lives. In 1954, a social psychologist named Leon Festinger suggested that human beings had a tendency to evaluate themselves via comparison to others. How smart am I? How attractive? How cultured? Wealthy? Are my opinions okay — not too hot and not too cold compared to my peers? Known as social comparison theory, the idea is that, for better or for worse, we tend to rate our own personal value vis-a-vis how we feel we score versus others.

For anyone suffering from insecurity (and who doesn't have some?), the often inflated picture we have of how well others are doing can pave the road to low self-esteem. The extent to which we sense others as having more, doing more, accomplishing more, enjoying more, the less we appreciate what we have and the greater our level of envy.

It was bad enough in 1954 when Festinger presented his theory, when we derived our sense of the other from relatively innocuous sources like *Life Magazine* and whatever we happened to fantasize about the lives of celebrities. Fast forward to the information age.

Them and Me-dia

According to some estimates, the average person now spends close to 2 hours — and teens up to 9 hours! — a day on social media. While social scientists are just now beginning to calculate the catastrophic impact that such trends are having on the emotional and mental health of young people, our specific concern here relates to the consequences for marriage. The problem is that social media provides social comparison on steroids. Few of our "friends" post pictures of themselves dressed for a regular day and doing the mundane activities that make up most hours of our lives. On the contrary, the pictures reveal some fantasy or idealized version of themselves. Everyone just looks so good, and they're all having such a good time. Every man so fascinating. Every woman so thin and sensual. And all those happy couples! Such exciting lives! So much passion!

Whatever you may have thought prior to social media about things that were missing in your marriage — he could be more passionate and interesting, she could lose a couple of pounds — the constant barrage of unreal images of others at their unnatural best is enough to lead a spouse to despair. I never realized just how bad and boring and lacking heat my marriage truly is! Each newsfeed, every instagram, any snapchat offers an opportunity to devalue my own life and even more so my spouse, who of course is holding me back from all that. Suffice to say that trying to build your marriage amidst social comparison of this magnitude is akin to placing more and more weights on my shoulder as I try to climb an already steep mountain.

Rags...

Having laid out the pattern of relationship reality, we're still not out of the woods. In our experience as counselors, we have seen certain issues arise repetitively in the marriages of our students that frankly shocked us when we first encountered them.

NOT A PARTNERSHIP

Jordan and Annie[35] were a match made in heaven. Both were nurtured by loving and healthy families in middle America, had no traumatic experiences in childhood, enjoyed good health, and had advanced degrees in business (him) and social work (her). More important still, both took life seriously and spent time systematically developing mature outlooks on life and love. Each had a strong track record of identifying and working through character flaws that might serve as liabilities in marriage and parenting. And their chemistry was amazing. In short, pretty much all you need to ensure a happy and nurturing marriage.

Surprisingly, as we stayed in touch with them, we began to notice something worrisome. The happy look of youth and optimism began to fade, replaced by what appeared to be a certain aging. The birth of their first child, with its explosion of emotion and celebration in the early weeks, seemed only to exacerbate the tension and "aging" as the first three years rolled by. Yet both claimed they were fine and didn't need any help.

When they finally did reach out it appeared that their happiness together had nearly ended. Certain negative patterns had developed. Jordan was now more critical of Annie. Annie had begun to nag Jordan. They still professed love and commitment; no one had cheated, there was no violence or abuse. Just a certain light that had gone out. The more we spoke with them about the dynamic in their relationship, the more we heard about a certain reality that had developed that we would later encounter in many other couples in their early years of marriage as well.

---

35. In all the stories that derive from our counseling experience, we have changed names and minor details to protect the privacy of the individuals involved.

Money was tight. Jordan had to travel frequently. Still young in his career in programming, it was a stretch to make ends meet. They lived in a tiny one-bedroom apartment, which became even tinier with the arrival of their daughter. Annie was left to fend for herself with her baby, the housework, the shopping, and trying to work several hours a day while the baby was in daycare. There wasn't enough money left for much extra babysitting or housekeeping help. There was little family help since neither set of parents lived nearby.

The typical evening played out as follows: As Jordan arrived home, Annie was beginning to collapse from the long and arduous day. She usually did manage to have dinner on the table, but they almost never ate together; she ate earlier so that when Jordan arrived home he could watch the baby for a few minutes while she rested and read a magazine to regain her sanity. Then she bathed the baby and put her to sleep while Jordan did the dishes and helped straighten up the house. As Jordan spent a few minutes answering his business emails, Annie showered and fell into bed for the night, or at least until the baby cried. Only to start again the next day in an exhausting and monotonous cycle.

Several tell-tale signs emerged:

1. They did not have any help in the house
2. There was no money to "spoil" each other
3. Date nights rarely if ever happened, let alone vacations together
4. Intimacy had become infrequent and stale

And all this from a couple who actually were loving and committed and giving.

Jordan and Annie experienced a common stress factor: limited financial resources. Money pressures can drag down every part of life. The stress itself sucks up mental energy with anguish and anxiety. Add to that the husband's guilt of not providing properly or the wife's resentment over not being provided for. The lack of sufficient funds also creates the additional difficulties of no help with keeping the house in order or taking care of the children, cramped quarters that crush the sense of space and tranquility, no extra funds to go out and live it up, no fancy presents. In short, the lack of money drains life of its sense of enjoyment. It surely leaves precious little energy to invest in making my spouse feel loved and cherished.

The irony is that Jordan and Annie, like many serious and committed couples, actually did achieve a certain *technical* level of giving (e.g., he works and pays the bills to support them, she takes care of their baby and does their laundry). While exemplary, necessary, and important, such technical giving alone — checking the box, in a way — in the absence of fresh and positive energy throughout the week won't cut it. Ironically, in the absence of regular emotional re-fostering, such task-based giving often leads couples down the treacherous path of the unhappy partnership, with each side feeling underappreciated ("she has no gratitude for what I do") and resentful ("I'm doing my job, but he isn't holding up *his* side of the bargain"). In short, technical giving without renewal can rapidly drive young couples into old marriages.

...TO RICHES

We might be tempted to think that a high-paying career (or two) would solve the problem. Think again.

Five years after their marriage, Jordan got the break that turned the family's finances around. The software company he worked for landed contracts with several Fortune 500 companies, and Jordan was promoted to manage the teams. Although this meant relocating to a new community, it also meant moving into a three-bedroom, single-family house, getting two company cars, and doubling his salary and bonus. His new position more than paid the bills; it left over plenty for lots of help in the house, nice things, clothing, jewelry, vacations, and charitable endeavors.

At first, their relationship was carried by the high of their good fortune. They shared the excitement and joy of suddenly being able to afford those things that helped them spend more time together. But not much time passed before each side again began to confide in us regarding their lack of satisfaction with the relationship. Annie found Jordan extremely preoccupied with his business life. Sometimes, his workday left him so stressed and exhausted that their time together on weekends seemed to be no more than recuperation periods — brief pit stops that led right back to the racetrack of a career in the fast lane.

Jordan, stimulated by the challenge of his work, surrounded by female colleagues who always looked and smelled and acted their best, began viewing Annie in a more negative light. Why didn't she always look tip-top? What was she accomplishing with all those free hours while he toiled? Annie for her part felt alone and overly stressed and underappreciated with the responsibility of the kids and home falling on her alone. She became lonely and distant, while he, also feeling underappreciated for how hard he was working to provide for his family, pulled away more into his own world, finding more satisfaction in work than in his stressful domestic life.

In their new lifestyle, unlike their earlier one, there was plenty of money for help in the house and for vacations. However, the tell-tale signs appeared here as well:

1. No time for date nights
2. Little or no intimacy
3. Insufficient appreciation of each other's contributions

Choose your poison

Driven by financial and logistical stresses in the first few years of their marriage, Jordan and Annie's relationship grew old. In the next few years, after his lucky break, their relationship, despite the availability of resources, emptied out of love and passion as too little time together conspired with languishing appreciation of each other's roles and accomplishments. Seemingly, neither rags nor riches provide an appropriate medium within which to incubate love, passion, concern, and respect. We have watched relationships become stale in any context.

What are the lethal common denominators that the rich and poor share?

- Insufficient time for each other
- Distractions that ruin the time they do share
- Infrequent intimacy

Moves that don't work

Before we lay out a practical strategy, let's mention a few things that, from all we've seen in our own work with couples, *don't* work.

A 2013 article in the *Huffington Post* entitled, "How to Keep Your Marriage Fresh,"[36] lists five strategies for keeping the "lust" alive in marriage beyond the two-year romance phase. They include:

1. Move. Keep changing your environment, if not a new home then remodeling to make the old place feel new
2. Go on separate vacations
3. Get a new look, for example, the removal or addition of facial hair, or a new style of dress
4. Have a quarterly update. Take a mini vacation, or spend the night together in a hotel while someone watches the kids
5. [We'll summarize the final suggestion more or less as:] Get involved in some type of illicit or semi-illicit activity with the knowledge of, or in front of your spouse, to arouse jealousy and create excitement

While we do believe that the author captured the crucial need to maintain freshness in marriage, we highly doubt the effectiveness of his proposals. While such strategies may rekindle the flame for a few nights, we believe these roads all end in cul-de-sacs, with the exception of the "quarterly

---

36. Nelkin, Stacey. "How to Keep Your Marriage Fresh." *The Huffington Post.* March 4, 2013, www.huffingtonpost.com/stacey-nelkin/how-to-keep-your-marriage_1_b_2286208.html.

update" which we'll discuss in more detail below. Changing homes (#1) and looks (#3) have no greater chance of surviving the short-term than did the original romance, even less; they certainly don't move a relationship forward. Separate vacations (#2) may serve to awaken the senses of the traveling spouse, but they also serve to separate the couple's intimate connection of shared moments, creating a longer-term divide. As to the illicit activity scenario (#5), any temporary arousal is very likely to create a much more pernicious long-term resentment and lack of trust. Honestly, how many husbands or wives will ever lose the image of their spouse violating the core privacy and sanctity of their intimacy by flirting or otherwise being involved with another man or woman?

Love is boring?

So wait, are you telling me that love is simply meant to be just one long, commitment-based, but *boring* relationship? No real solutions? That's what the Almighty had in mind for us?

The answer is a resounding "no"!

The trick, and work, of life is to seek and create meaningful moments and periods of passion and inspiration throughout the stage-two period of marriage. Harnessing those emotions provides the reserves we can draw upon to continue building a stronger and more beautiful reality and relationship, even when we're not in a euphoric state. The road back to Eden is built on that pattern.

As we'll see in all four pillars of building your marriage, each is really just another opportunity for, and practical expression of, giving. By practicing and repeating numerous achievable modes of giving — from spending to speaking to helping to providing intimacy — giving will, over time, become second nature. That's how the human changes herself. Practicing in an outward manner ultimately builds an inner reality. For example, someone who is stingy need only practice continually putting his hand in his pocket and giving away money; eventually he'll become a more generous person. Once the bad trait has been transformed into a good one, the giving can become more balanced and discriminating. It's a classic, and profound, case of fake it 'til you make it. But that's how we change.

PRACTICAL STEPS: PRIORITIZE YOUR SPOUSE

The quest for freshness lies in three primary strategies which, from our experience, cannot but produce fruit. The insight does not lie in the fact that these areas are important. We all know that. The trick is to take the steps to build them into our relationship with consistency. We'll first summarize three key strategies before going into more detail.

1. Make time for each other

Our lives are busier than ever. Few professions that offer upside allow for true work-life separation. The best model most of us can strive for is work-life *integration*. Yet we all know that a relationship needs both quality time *and* quantity time. Without spending time focused only on our marriage, we drift apart. We'll lay out the case for two separate types of focused time: inviolable weekly date nights and quarterly short-but-sweet overnight getaways. Longer vacations should be considered a bonus.

2. Spend on your marriage

Money is often, if not always, tight. Yet most of us manage to spend a little something on whatever it is we love (just check yourself on your latest gadget, your watch, your gym membership, your purse, your shoes — all of which somehow crept past the budget overload). The real leverage in your spending lies in the relationship. Yes, we all feel that we spend on our spouses already — the car, the phone, clothing. But more direct benefit derives from spending money either to make my spouse's life easier (such as investing in cleaning help) or making my spouse feel more special (a gift, a massage, a facial). In other words, the next time you find money to spend on something you love, make sure it's your spouse.

3. Prioritize intimacy

Perhaps no area of marriage offers more energy and happiness per unit of investment than plain old physical intimacy — in the context of a loving relationship. It may be self-evident, but research shows that couples who have more frequent sexual encounters report happier and more fulfilling marriages well into old age.[37] Yet, not surprisingly, in our busy and self-engrossed lives, intimacy usually falls apart over the course of a marriage. According to one survey, the

---

[37]. Galinsky, Adena M., and Linda J. Waite. "Sexual Activity and Psychological Health As Mediators of the Relationship Between Physical Health and Marital Quality." *The Journals of Gerontology*. May 1, 2014, doi.org/10.1093/geronb/gbt165.

frequency of intimacy experienced by married couples aged 18-29 falls by about a quarter during the next decade, and then by another 20% during the following 10 years, or by nearly 40% in total.[38] Like any other important arena for giving and building the relationship, intimacy must be prioritized. While not separable from the commitment to date nights and vacations, the powerful role of sexuality in keeping marriage fresh warrants its own discussion.

Strategy #1: Make time for each other

Once upon a time, when your grandparents were young, couples spent time together. Lots of it. I Love Lucy time. Leave it to Beaver time. Dad would come home in the late afternoon; he'd sit with his pipe, paper, and whisky. Mom would be putting the finishing touches on the casserole and the chocolate chip cookies. The evening would be spent in a relaxed series of activities — dinner with the kids, some catch in the backyard, back in for homework, a solid hour and a half of TV before bed. Time.

In our generation, time has evaporated. And what precious extra time we do have has been almost entirely absorbed by technology through endless televised and online entertainment, social media, and a bottomless pit of information and activity. Little wonder that we've become overly reliant on "quality time" as quantity has all but vanished. "Hey! Let's make that 20 minutes before we collapse and fall asleep [or get started on Netflix] really count!"

---

38. Smith, Tom W. "American Sexual Behavior: Trends, Socio-Demographic Differences, and Risk Behavior." *National Opinion Research Center*, University of Chicago. March 2006, www.norc.org/PDFs/Publications/AmericanSexualBehavior2006.pdf.

While there is little doubt that quality time can be powerful and restorative, it doesn't suffice on its own. Couples have to work to expand quality time to include more (even if limited by life's realities) *quantity* time. Combining quality with quantity allows me to *prioritize* my spouse and helps us to stay passionately and lovingly connected.

SAVE THE DATE!
MAKING DATE NIGHT PART OF YOUR SCHEDULE

In our work with students, we have found few things more valuable in keeping marriage alive than a weekly date night etched in-stone. Indeed, with many couples, including those whose stories we summarized above, part of the solution to their quandary was to begin committing time regularly to each other away from life's myriad other demands, involvements, and activities. Something so simple, obvious, and relationship-strengthening, date night nonetheless remains elusive for most couples. It's hard to come by hard statistics, but some survey data show that as much as 45% of couples "rarely" go out together, fewer than a fifth manage about once a month, and only 16% manage once a week.[39] That's despite the fact that date nights are an important arrow in the quiver of anyone working to keep marriage fresh amidst a busy, stressed, and distracted life.

---

39. Redbookmag.com, February 2010, page 90.

HIGH PAYOFF

In 2012, researchers Brad Wilcox and Jeffrey Dew from the University of Virginia's National Marriage Project released a report called the Date Night Opportunity.[40] Among the powerful findings:

- *Husbands' and wives' reports of couple time were associated with higher relationship quality.* Husbands and wives who engaged in couple time with their mates at least once a week were approximately 3.5 times more likely to report being "very happy" in their marriages, compared to those who enjoyed less quality time with their spouse.

- *Couple time seems to foster more stable marriages.* Spouses who experience high levels of couple time are significantly less likely to report that they are prone to divorce. For example, wives who reported having couple time less than once a week were nearly four times more likely to report above-average levels of divorce proneness, compared to wives who enjoyed couple time at least once a week with their husbands. Husbands who reported spending less than once a week in couple time were 2.5 times more likely to be divorce prone, compared to husbands who had couple time with their wives at least once a week.

---

40. Baumgardner, Julie. "Is Date Night for Married Couples a Thing of the Past?" *Times Free Press.* October 18, 2015, www.timesfreepress.com/news/life/entertainment/story/2015/oct/18/first-things-first-date-night-married-couples/330728.

❦ *Couple time is associated with better intimate lives.* Wives who spend couple time with their husbands at least once a week are 3.5 times more likely to enjoy above-average levels of sexual satisfaction, compared to wives who have couple time less than once a week. Likewise, husbands who spend more couple time with their wives are 3.3 times more likely to enjoy above-average levels of sexual satisfaction, compared to their peers who have couple time less than once a week.

KID STUFF

Nor did the data suggest that it's only parents preoccupied with their kids who need time away. On the contrary, Professors Wilcox and Dew found that "couple time was equally important for both types of married couples."

Needless to say, once baby arrives, parents have to work a lot harder to make date nights happen. But the payoff is high: the researchers found that "new parents who did not reduce their couple time together after the arrival of a baby were markedly less likely to experience a decline in marital quality.... For instance...new parents who saw their couple time decline across the transition to parenthood were about two times more likely to experience a decline in marital quality, compared to new parents who kept up their couple time."

DRIVING TO AND FROM DATES

How can something so simple and inexpensive and involving so little time produce such high benefits? Wilcox and

Dew list five key drivers to the power of date nights.

- *Communication.* Without time and space to communicate — beyond the typical logistics that over time come to dominate spousal conversation — we lose track of each other. Date nights offer a chance to remove distractions related to kids and jobs and everything else. Over coffee we can get back to sharing our dreams, our concerns, our interests, and our lives. The fact that it's in person and private makes it that much more special. Humans aren't static. We change and grow. Without shared private time we become more and more disconnected from each other's development, in the process becoming ever more peripheral to one another. "Date nights may help partners and spouses to 'stay current' with each other's lives and offer one another support for meeting these challenges."

- *Novelty.* Most couples experience a decline in relationship quality after a few years, partly because they become habituated to one another and are more likely to take their relationship and each other for granted. The initial excitement associated with getting to know a person, growing in intimacy, and trying new things as a couple can disappear as the two people settle into a routine. By contrast, a growing body of research suggests that couples who engage in novel activities that are fun, active, or otherwise arousing — from hiking to dancing to travel to card games — enjoy higher levels of relationship quality. Thus, date nights should foster this higher quality, especially insofar as couples use them to engage in exciting, active, or unusual activities. In other words, couples may be particularly likely to benefit from a regular date night if they use it as an opportunity to do more than that old standby: dinner and a movie. It is also important that they choose activities that represent a balance of each partner's interests, rather than tending to do things (novel or not) that are desired more by the same partner each time.

- *Eros.* Most contemporary relationships begin with an element of eros — that romantic love that is linked to passion, excitement, and an overwhelming sense of attraction to one's beloved. Without proper investment of time and energy and giving, the emotional and physical manifestations of erotic love tend to decline in most couples. Date nights allow couples to focus on their relationship, to share feelings, to engage in romantic activities with one another, and to try new things. The regular rekindling of that romantic spark can be very helpful in sustaining the fires of love over the long haul. All of these things can foster higher levels of sexual satisfaction in their marriage.

- *Commitment.* Husbands and wives are more likely to enjoy stable, high-quality relationships when they experience a strong sense of commitment to one another and to their relationship. Specifically, partners who put one another first, who steer clear of other romantic opportunities, and who cultivate a strong sense of "we-ness" or togetherness are markedly happier than are less-committed couples. Date nights may solidify an expectation of commitment among couples by fostering a sense of togetherness, by allowing partners to signal to one another — as well as friends and family — that they take their relationship seriously, and by furnishing them with opportunities to spend time with one another, to communicate, and to enjoy fun activities together.

- *De-stress.* Stress is one of the biggest threats to a strong marriage. Stress related to work, finances, parenthood, or illness can prove corrosive to a relationship by causing one or both partners to become irritable, withdrawn, violent, or otherwise difficult to live with. Date nights may be helpful for relieving stress on couples, as they allow them to enjoy time with one another apart from the pressing concerns of their ordinary life. Moreover, date nights may allow spouses to extend emotional support to one another in times of trial. For all these reasons, date nights may help couples by providing them with a buffer or an escape from the stresses that confront them or time to engage in collaborative coping that can reduce those stresses.

Tech-free zone!

We need to add that none of these benefits will accrue if the attention I should be paying to my spouse (and vice-versa) gets divided on the date. How many times have we been shocked to see a couple sitting at a table together in a restaurant while each is fully absorbed in texting? It's sort of an electronic adultery session as the other spouse looks on (or enjoys an escape to her own cyber adventure). We strongly recommend that phones be set aside and silenced to all outsiders save for the babysitter. Otherwise, you might as well stay home.

For the babysitting (or financially) challenged...

Many times our students have complained to us that they simply can't get out for a date night due to logistical or financial constraints. Reliable babysitters aren't always available. Money is tight. For those occasions we recommend having an "in" date night, which, when properly done, loses nothing vis-a-vis "out" nights. Put the kids to bed. Place the smartphones on silent. Turn the TV off. Buy Chinese or cook some pasta. Open that bottle of wine you've been saving. Dim the lights. Soft music.

Date night doesn't depend on where we are; it is solely a function of how we relate to each other. A short walk together holding hands. Grabbing a quick lunch together amidst a hectic day. Coffee (with or without dessert). Again, the *what* is nearly irrelevant. What matters is making my spouse my complete and total priority for that weekly time without distraction. If the evening ends with intimacy, it's a bonus!

In stone

It may seem a bit hokey, but we often ask our student couples to sign a date night contract (usually on the back of a napkin that we pick up in the cafe where we're meeting together to discuss their marriage). Each of them signs and we hold a photo for safekeeping. Key points:

1. We'll make a date night every Tuesday night (it could be any night, but we like Tuesday because it is already into the week, yet early enough to reschedule for Wednesday or Thursday if an emergency comes up).
2. We won't wait until Tuesday afternoon to plan it.
3. If possible, we'll line up regular recurring babysitting.
4. Every other week we'll take turns planning the evening.
5. We'll move mountains to make sure nothing interrupts the night — and if something unexpected does happen, we'll shoot for Wednesday.
6. If one or both of us has to travel we'll do our best to Skype (with video) for half an hour from wherever we are (Skype is better than phone since it doesn't allow anyone to multitask when they should be focusing on each other).

X _____ (her)
X _____ (him)

You get the point. Plan it (and if you're out of ideas, Google shows 49,600,000...). Enshrine it. Defend it. Enjoy it together!

Always be in planning mode!

The power of short vacations

Can't even remember...
According to a 2010 survey of 2,000 women, 40% of spouses "can't even remember" the last time they left town together without their kids. Fewer than a third take a trip once a year, and a de minimis 3% get away frequently.[41]

It's a mistake.

Vacations are critical for our emotional, mental, and physical health. The chronic stress and sleep deprivation that all but a few wealthy heirs experience can cause any number of physical ailments, negatively affecting our circulation, blood pressure, digestion, and immunity. Beyond the merely physical, prolonged stress and poor sleep contribute to increased levels of irritability, depression, and anxiety.[42] Bad enough in isolation, the maladies can prove lethal in a relationship.

British researcher Scott McCabe noted that vacations' "personal benefits have been found to include: rest and recuperation from work; provision of new experiences leading to a broadening of horizons and the opportunity for learning and intercultural communication; promotion of peace and understanding; personal and social development; visiting friends and relatives; religious pilgrimage and health; and, subjective well-being."[43]

---

41. Spencer, Amy, and Lindsey Palmer. "Is Your Love Life Normal? Our Most Revealing Survey Yet." *Redbook*. January 10, 2010, www.redbookmag.com/love-sex/advice/a5816/revealing-relationship-survey.
42. Krauss Whitbourne, Susan. "The Importance of Vacations to Our Physical and Mental Health." *Psychology Today*. June 22, 2010, www.psychologytoday.com/intl/blog/fulfillment-any-age/201006/the-importance-vacations-our-physical-and-mental-health.
43. Krauss Whitbourne, S.

We know what you're thinking right now — no one needs proof that vacations are great, especially when it comes to my physical and mental health, and with respect to maintaining freshness in my marriage in particular. *But there's simply no time, no money and no one to watch our kids even if we can get away!*

You are correct. But there's a solution.

Make it short

Psychologists are beginning to catch onto the notion that more frequent, but *shorter*, vacations provide an optimal solution and leave people happier than the longer but more infrequent variety. By short, we mean short. Even a night away, even five minutes away, is a game changer. Rather than using your vacation days in a last ditch attempt to save the relationship once a year — with an incredible amount of attendant financial and logistical stress — we highly recommend a totally different strategy of shorter and sweeter.

Author and behavioral psychologist Dan Ariely of Duke University gives part of the rationale: "On a long vacation, day seven is less good than day one because it's not as exciting. That's why, in general, going away four times [a year] provides more benefit than you would expect, and going away for one week provides less benefit than you would expect."[44] That is, before we even get to the issue of doability, we have to acknowledge that longer vacations suffer from the law of declining marginal returns, with each successive

---

44. Roberts, Laura. "Short Breaks Make People Happier Than One Long Holiday, Psychologists Claim." *The Telegraph*. August 15, 2010, www.telegraph.co.uk/travel/travelnews/7946668/Short-breaks-make-people-happier-than-one-long-holiday-psychologists-claim.html.

day providing less and less incremental joy. Researchers at the University of Canterbury in New Zealand found that "the duration of a vacation appeared to have negligible effects on remembered happiness."[45]

Experience vs. memory

The conceptual well of thinking underlying our push for short vacations runs deep. In a famous TED Talk,[46] Nobel laureate Daniel Kahneman distinguished between aspects that make up our psyche and identity: the *experiencing* self and the *remembering* self. The experiencing self, well, experiences life on a moment-by-moment basis. According to Kahneman, the psychological "present" lasts for about 3 seconds — adding up to about 20,000 moments of experience per day or around 600 million over the course of a lifetime — most of which are lost without a trace to the remembering self. It's the experiencing self to whom the doctor asks: "Does this hurt?" The remembering self is the story teller (to others, yes, but more importantly, to yourself), the one that processes and judges and threads the experiences and moments. To this one the doctor asks: "How have you been feeling? Did the diet help?"

While something like a vacation is experienced moment by moment — the tastes and sights and sounds and feelings — by the experiencing self, the vacation is actually

---

45. Kemp, Simon, et al. "A Test of the Peak-end Rule With Extended Autobiographical Events." *Memory & Cognition*. January, 2008, doi.org/10.3758/MC.36.1.132.
46. Kahneman, Daniel. "The Riddle of Experience vs. Memory." *TED Talks*. February, 2010, www.ted.com/talks/daniel_kahneman_the_riddle_of_experience_vs_memory/transcript.

remembered and cherished (or not) by the remembering self. The latter is the part of you that can enjoy an entire vacation moment by moment for two weeks (or a symphony, note by note) and then say it was all ruined by the disastrous trip home (or the screeching sound at the end of the recording).

In most of life, it is our remembering self that takes precedence and creates the happiness or lack thereof in its assessment of the now-gone experiences. And much of that is itself determined by *changes,* or by the sharpness of the emotional content in the moment experienced.

When it comes to vacations, Kahneman's insight is that the two selves are poorly aligned. Says Kahneman: "We go on vacations, to a very large extent, in the service of our remembering self." Meaning, it's not so much the feeling of the actual moments that we live through, it's rather the impression on our memories and sense of well-being that the trip makes upon us. From that standpoint, a two-week vacation may actually add little to a one-week vacation. Why? Because it's more of the same. As Kahneman says, "no new memories added; you have not changed the story." The actual emotional imprint was made with the newness of the experience. Again, declining marginal returns. So despite the fact that in terms of *experience*, two weeks is twice as good, that extra week is actually not additive at all to the impact on the happiness, well-being, and loving memories associated with the trip.

The take-away? Short is just as sweet!

Keep planning

Shorter and more frequent vacations hold another strong advantage over the big but infrequent vacation: more planning and anticipation. As Professor Ariely from Duke puts it: Think about the timeline. You have the time before the vacation; you have the time during the vacation; and you have the time after the vacation. Before the vacation is the time that you get to think about the vacation and anticipate it. During the vacation is when you actually enjoy the vacation, and afterwards it's the time that you savor. You look back; you think about it and so on.

"From those three periods, which is the shortest? The actual vacation. In fact, when you think about the vacation, you shouldn't think just about the vacation, you should also think about anticipation and also think about memory. And I can tell you that personally we've gone to some vacations with my family that, at the moment, were not fantastic. At the moment you would say that we climbed some mountains; it was difficult, it was complex, and so on. So the actual vacation itself, every moment of it was not exactly joyful, but reflecting on it backwards has been just amazing. So that's one thing about vacation: you really want to think about the whole experience and what vacations are going to actually enrich your life and become input for memory for years to come and not just something that is good for its own sake."[47]

---

47. Ariely, Dan. "Two Reasons Your Vacations Aren't Making You Happy." *Big Think.* July 31, 2015, bigthink.com/videos/dan-ariely-on-choosing-the-best-vacation.

The thrill of planning the next vacation together is a powerful driver of freshness for a couple. It doesn't need a lot of time. Those 15 minutes we grab every night for a week while picking the place, finding the right hotel, thinking about where we'll eat and what we might see drives a special closeness and shared excitement and anticipation, not only regarding the trip itself, but about the way we will enjoy it together.

Most startling, a group of Dutch researchers[48] actually discovered that of the three distinct time zones in the creation of a vacation — planning, experiencing, remembering — it is actually the planning period that provides the most intense impact on happiness. The group examined whether vacationers differ in happiness, compared to those not going on holiday, and if a holiday trip boosts post-trip happiness. Here's what they found: Vacationers reported a higher degree of pre-trip happiness, compared to non-vacationers, possibly because they are anticipating their holiday. Only a very relaxed holiday trip boosts vacationers' happiness further after return. Generally, there is no difference between vacationers' and non-vacationers' post-trip happiness.

Think about that — when we get home, we might not be a lot better off than had we not gone, unless it's a really good vacation. But the experience of planning a vacation together, which can last longer than the actual vacation, *does* boost happiness!

---

48. Nawijn, Jeroen, et al. "Vacationers Happier, but Most not Happier After a Holiday." *Applied Research in Quality of Life*. March, 2010, doi.org/10.1007/s11482-009-9091-9.

Getting the max from mini

For many strapped and overly burdened young couples, even one-week vacations appear out of reach realistically. Fortunately, we have found an alternative, one we've seen used with great success. We call it the mini-vacation. One night away, sometimes just a day. Close by, inexpensive. The key to gaining the relationship boost lies in the excitement of the planning (which, as we've seen, can yield stronger and longer-lasting impact than the actual vacation), and the excitement, closeness, and freshness wrought through the shared private, passionate time.

There's no need to travel far. That little inn down the road is perfectly fine. If you live near a big city, try a night in the city; if you're downtown, try uptown. City too expensive? Try the B&B (or Airbnb) in the nearest village. The point is that it isn't your usual surroundings; it's just the two of you. The almost total lack of stress in getting away for such a short time helps ensure the lingering effect — no long flights with attendant delays and bad food. Just back in the car and home in five minutes.

If all else fails

Babysitting overnight generally proves the biggest challenge, but one that can be overcome with some ingenuity. And if all else fails, make it a one-day vacation. Rent the hotel room, pick up a pizza (and perhaps the wine bottle). Take a good book or magazine along. Plan it, enjoy it, and create a powerful shared memory of emotion-laden content.

As a practical matter, subscribe to a good travel app and set the parameters to inform you anytime a great cheap deal comes up in your target area. You can seek the every-three-month weekend getaway or the single nighter or the day vacation. *The point is to keep it going, and always to be in the mode of planning your next vacation together.*

Strategy #2: Spend on your marriage!

The classic male hates to spend money. On the contrary, *having* money is where the real power lies, since with it I can buy anything! The classic female loves to spend money. Just ask your wife and she'll tell you how foolish it is to have money and not use it — after all, if you don't actually buy anything, then you have *nothing*. But just ask your husband, and he'll prove what a waste of money that was, since it means we won't be able to afford what we really want when we really want it. And so on and so on.

We won't solve this cosmic dilemma for you, but we would like to elucidate a certain principle. Spending money can help grease the wheels of your marriage, providing the highest investment return we can imagine (higher even than Bitcoin). Many problems in daily marital life — drudgery, stress, overwhelming household activities, inability to leave the kids or to distract them — derive from a lack of willingness to spend, despite the fact that fairly small amounts of targeted outlays can solve significant issues.

HELP PREPARE FOR MARRIAGE

Tod still remembers the day he told his rabbi-mentor that he had become engaged. Before the Jewish phrase *"mazal tov!"* (part congratulations, part good luck, part blessing) was pronounced, his rabbi took his hand and said: "Make sure you always spend money to have help in the house.

Sacrifice on other things you need for that. That way your wife will always feel like a human being." Only then did he add a hearty *"mazal tov!"*

SAVE LATER

The tension between saving and spending threatens to upend every marriage just about every moment until that tipping point where incomes begin to outpace spending by a healthy margin. Usually, it's husband/saving versus wife/spending, but not always. It doesn't matter. From our experience, savings in those very early years, when money is tight, usually add up to very little. They certainly are outweighed by the impact of loosening the strings to make life more bearable. The ironic and tragic outcome occurs when the struggling savers, who forgo every convenience to provide for those college and retirement funds, create so much stress that the money anyway gets spent on long-term therapy, if not divorce. It is the very definition of penny-wise and pound-foolish.

By way of self-test, try to take a small and short inventory of the things you somehow did find the money for, despite that need to contribute to the college fund. New iPhone (absolutely necessary!). Good seats for the playoffs. That priced-out-of-range pair of shoes. We somehow do find ways to spend on things we really want, irrespective of their actual importance and necessity, and despite the siren song of the need to save. All we're advocating is thinking more about your spouse and relationship when allocating.

Who, what and where (the why is obvious)

The fairly obvious priorities in recurring expenditures lie in areas like:

- Household cleaning help
- Babysitting

When it comes to capital outlays, the highest returns are found with respect to:

- A car (or, if more relevant, a taxi fund)
- A dishwasher
- Laundry machines
- Microwave

Let's think of those as the drudgery dampeners — they sort of let you out of the dungeon. However, they don't help you reach the promised land of well-being. For that, we have to loosen the strings still further for such necessary luxuries as:

- Gym memberships
- Enrichment classes
- Petty cash for small-time, non-necessity linked shopping

Spending accounts

While we're all too familiar with the savings accounts, we're much less familiar with targeted spending accounts. For early stages — or as long as it's tight — we encourage our students to set up little accounts for things like date nights and mini-vacations. If you find yourself either too disorganized, or too emotionally unwilling, to make those weekly or bi-weekly (whenever the paycheck arrives) deposits into the old cookie jar, then automate the process. Create a plan for direct deposits into a second shared bank account. Sometimes couples are shocked when a few months later they suddenly have enough for that overnight in the city. The payoff is high.

MAKE A WISH (AND DON'T BOWL HER OVER)
In a classic episode of The Simpsons, Marge's birthday arrives. Ever the thoughtful husband, Homer gives her a present that he has spent time planning for. A bowling ball, with his name on it....

Similarly, wives in particular often complain to us that their husbands usually blow it when it comes to presents. Assuming he doesn't forget the birthday or anniversary altogether (for shame!), the gift nonetheless can come out lame (think bowling ball), if he even remembered to buy one.

Sensing avoidable catastrophes in the making, we created an informal focus group of about 20 young wives and asked them for ideas about how to improve a husband's gift-giving acumen. Their top recommendation? Let each spouse create a gift wishlist on, for example, Amazon. Fill it with things you'd like that are cheap, mid-range, and more expensive. Make sure there's an assortment. Maybe for good luck purchase Amazon Prime in case he waits until the last minute.... Such a simple and elegant solution. All the pain of having to spend unavailable time, and the anxiety of his not really knowing what she likes, or of the recipient having to explain that while really pink paisleys would go so nicely with that grey suit, yet it may just be too forward a look, so with sadness I must return it....

The only real loss is the excitement of the spontaneous purchase, and the warmth generated when he discovers that she really went out of her way to go shopping for him. But at least part of that loss will be mitigated by actually getting a present on time that fits your actual needs, wishes, and body.

Strategy #3: Prioritize intimacy

BODY AND SOUL

Jewish wisdom recognizes that each human being is made up of both physical and spiritual components, each comprising a set of needs and desires. The ultimate goal is to harmonize the two sides, not to starve either, while ultimately giving precedence, or a leadership role, to the spiritual side. Not to stifle the physical, but to enlist it in the service of a higher set of goals. Focusing only on my, and my spouse's, physical needs, we'll tend to use and objectify each other. On the other hand, pretending we're angels will starve us of the incredible benefits of providing and enjoying physical pleasure for and with each other. Our emotional and intellectual selves long for respect and love and care. Our bodies crave sensual gratification.

An *integrated* being seeks, and deserves, all of it. At times emphasis will be on one or the other, but they can always remain connected. Love and respect create the deepest desire for physical closeness which, when properly given, will only enhance and build the love in the most virtuous of cycles. That cycle, more than anything else, powers freshness and passion in marriage.

Make your marriage glow

Great physical intimacy in marriage can, *in the short-term*, also make up for shortcomings elsewhere, keeping freshness alive even in the face of threatening staleness. A normal, healthy adult often cannot achieve a sense of well-being without sexual satisfaction. And it's precisely when that satisfaction is provided by and with my spouse that it spills over to the rest of my being. That is, trying to take care of your sexual needs outside of the loving and committed relationship (whether through adultery or pornography) will more often than not leave you feeling even more empty than when you started, often within a moment of the peaking of that physical experience. But within the context of the relationship, physical pleasure plays an outsized role in generating well-being since it both expresses and feeds the higher aspects of self.

We all know that when we feel great and empowered and taken care of, the marital version of a hot meal and eight hours of sleep, everything simply looks better, is more tolerable and less irritating. When I'm stressed and tired and you step on my foot, look out for my swift reaction. If I'm feeling great and you step on my foot, no problem buddy, anyone can make a mistake. Becoming a consistent giver, one who speaks and acts with respect toward my spouse's emotional and spiritual reality, can take a long time to perfect. In the meanwhile, providing the frequency and intensity of physical pleasure my spouse needs can generate that positive and satisfied sense of self that will help smooth my rough edges while I strive to be a better giver.

Bolstering and helping to explain this classic tenet of Talmudic wisdom, a 2017 study of newlyweds found that partners experience a sexual "afterglow" that lasts for up to *48 hours*, and this afterglow is linked with relationship quality over the long-term.[49] That very afterglow, another way of characterizing a sense of well-being, truly helps us maintain passion and happiness in our marriage, even as other aspects of our spousal responsibilities have not been fully developed. No question that a kind word or deed makes a lasting impression, but 48 hours?! No wonder that intimacy is the true engine of marital happiness. Where else can you find a 48-fold (96-fold?) return on your investment?

Irony or tragedy?

On the one hand, a strong, consistent and passionate intimate life fuels the torch that can keep marital happiness burning long-term. On the other hand, it often seems like a lost cause. A large-scale study in 2015 found that marital passion peaks after just 12 months,[50] with the positive pattern of development of the first year dissolving into a lifelong dissolution thereafter. Twelve months! We suspect that may have a lot to do at least partly with the underlying reasons that people get married; namely, we fall in lust and mistake that as love. As we quickly discover when we come back down to earth, the lust simply can't last on its own with the same intensity. The irony, if not tragedy, defies description.

---

49. Meltzer, Andrea L., et al. "Quantifying the Sexual Afterglow." *Psychological Science*. March 16, 2017, doi.org/10.1177/0956797617691361.

50. Schmiedeberg, Claudia, and Jette Schröder. "Does Sexual Satisfaction Change With Relationship Duration?" *Archives of Sexual Behavior*. January, 2016, doi.org/10.1007/s10508-015-0587-0.

We're also losing interest!

Nor do the superficially-involved hold a monopoly over waning sexual passion. Even many serious, committed, and loving couples face the challenge. In work with our students, a group that generally marries with a strong sense of commitment and purpose (in addition to the all-critical physical attraction), the same concept has proven true.

Not only true but surprising — at least to the participants. Generally, the pre-marital male imagines that he will be chasing his wife around the house for the next 50 years given his highly passionate and testosterone-driven persona. In reality, the pursuer often gives way to *being pursued* in pretty short order. Within that first year, as he begins to slow, she often is just warming up, with her increased desire met with decreased satisfaction.

And of course sometimes both just seem to lose interest.

So while on the one hand, sexuality provides the most potent and leveraged investment available to build a marriage, on the other hand, it is literally falling apart before our eyes. Talk about a conundrum!

4 roads back (or forward)

You can overcome the odds. From what we've seen over and over, a combination of attitudinal change and the implementation of a few key strategies can save, rebuild, or sustain your intimate life, and in turn your marriage. Three dos, and one don't do. We'll take them in order:

    A. Make an effort

    B. Expand your definition of intimacy

C. Communicate regularly and clearly

D. Avoid activities that threaten the privacy and sanctity of the relationship

Let's make it clear from the outset: We see no need to provide any particular how-to for the bedroom. While Google search results on date night ideas number nearly 50 million, ideas on how to enhance intimate experience registers more than 200 million. So rather than compete with or summarize readily available ideas, we'll focus on the specific strategies and mindsets that can get you more regularly into the bedroom with more desire and more focus.

A. A FOR EFFORT

- *Steal time.* We sabotage ourselves from the beginning due to time constraints. Too little time rings as a constant refrain and excuse for my lack of effort, especially when it comes to investing in intimacy. Begin by telling yourself that you can make time and then start stealing it. Let someone else pick the kids up from school. Get takeout instead of making dinner. Wait until morning to take out the trash.

- *Give some of that time to yourself.* A few moments a day spent relaxing and reflecting help us to unwind and to reconnect with ourselves and our inner thoughts and emotions. If I'm disconnected from myself, how can I connect properly with my wife? Take that five minutes for a cup of coffee. If there are kids and chores, take turns with your spouse. Two relaxed people can then focus on each other.

- *Take care of yourself.* Many couples begin letting go of themselves after getting married. The pounds begin to pile up. The care in how they dress in front of each other begins to wane. Good health and fitness not only provide bodies that work better and have more stamina, they also enhance body awareness and a more positive self-image. Not to mention they keep you looking more like you did when you got married and the two of you were totally into each other.

- *Watch your weight!* Let's not lose sight of the reality, however superficial and radioactive the topic may seem. Besides the respect and admiration you had for each other when you met, you were also attracted to each other. If not, you'd have been friends but would never have married. Nothing kills attraction and drives resentment like the feeling that your attractive spouse has let himself go, especially when it comes to weight. That's exactly the feeling she has when his six-pack begins to look more like the cooler. Attraction is harmed since, well, he has become less attractive. Resentment, which is far more pernicious, grows, since she now feels either like he was faking it for the courtship, or worse, like he doesn't really care about how attractive he remains for her — or both. With more than 70% of over-20 adults classified by the CDC as overweight (or obese),[51] nearly everyone has to face the problem. The fact that obesity stats alone nearly double for the over 20-year-old crowd

---

51. Center for Disease Control and Prevention. "Obesity and Overweight." May 3, 2017, www.cdc.gov/nchs/fastats/obesity-overweight.htm.

(38%) versus the 12-19-year-old set (21%) suggests that many spouses will be in for a surprise when it comes to basic attractiveness. For most of us, implementing a diet and sticking to it is among life's most difficult challenges, but in the bedroom the payoff could not be higher, and for obvious reasons.

- *Keep up the appearance.* In case you'd like to take the self-test for how you may be contributing to the aging of your marriage, just ask yourself the following (painful) questions about how you've changed since the dating period until now:

    How careful were you to make an effort to look your best at all times? How about now?

    How much thought went into how you dressed, how you *smelled*?

    Here's another question: Do I spend as much time and care on how I look for my spouse as I do for work?

What exactly is the rationale for easing up? It's hard to justify, other than it's just not a key focus. If you get home earlier than your spouse, try showering and shaving and putting on some cologne or make-up, as the case may be. You'd have done it when you were dating. From our work with students it has the same (if not more) impact when you're married.

Before you complain that it's just an act, think about it — much of life is acting in order to give the other what he or she needs or wants. I act in front of my boss, yes; but also in front of my child, to whom I show a happy and excited face even after a bad day. My spouse will also be picked up by it. Again, the combination of showing effort and the higher level of attractiveness will result in more interest by your spouse, and will also serve as a subtle form of encouragement for reciprocation.

Have fun. As we've said repeatedly, couples grow "old" too fast. It is amazing what laughing and having fun can do for a relationship. Many couples we work with forget that amidst all the serious aspects and responsibilities of life as a couple or a family, *we're still basically the same cute kids we were before we got married. We still crave humor and a good time.* Couples that share leisure activities enjoy more love and less conflict than those who do not. By engaging in mutually enjoyable activities, you will feel more connected to your partner and forge a more intimate relationship. Having fun together builds intimacy in one of the strongest ways possible. How? By returning you emotionally and psychologically to a certain innocence that you once experienced together. That experience, whenever repeated, can give us the energy and broader perspective to shrug off some of life's stresses and difficulties. Fun activities include go-karting, mini-golf, or bowling. Follow this pathway when thinking about the date nights you are about to commit to.

Plan it. In a world of constant motion and business, nothing happens without proactively making the time for it. While we all treasure the excitement of spontaneity, when it comes to our intimate lives we can't leave it up to chance. Regular physical intimacy keeps both of you feeling wanted and desired. After the honeymoon phase of the relationship, keeping intimacy on top of the "to do" list can become a challenge if not a chore. So decide in advance, together, when it makes sense. Then make it happen! Write it into your diaries, or encode it on the kitchen calendar.

It may seem a contrivance, but, as we have seen, anticipation of a shared special time can be as important, if not more important, than the event itself. Don't leave your intimacy to chance and simply await the occasional spontaneous outburst (though don't squander those opportunities either!). However unromantic and businesslike it may sound, it's better to have *some* — even less-than-perfect — intimate encounters than none at all. It goes without saying that date night planning will overlap with this form of intimacy scheduling.

B. Expand your view of intimacy

We're used to thinking of intimacy as just another word for sexual relations. That's a mistake. Intimacy with my spouse should more properly include the gamut of uniquely and closely shared activities and experiences. Let's examine some of the ways an expanded vision of intimacy can feed and foster more closeness and sexuality.

Spoken intimacy. If your relationship is kept strong outside the bedroom, you have a good shot of keeping it strong in the bedroom. Life provides ample opportunity to make that happen.

- *Be smart with your phone.* Our definition of speech has been broadened to include text. Rather than using that smartphone as the thing that separates you when you're together, use it to connect you when you're apart. Make use of that calendar. Put on recurring reminders to text or call your spouse throughout the day. The simplest text asking how he's feeling, or how her meeting went, or better, telling her you can't wait to see her tonight, registers an impact and builds the all-important anticipation we're pushing for. You're anyway on the phone; divert your thumbs to texting her instead of your buddy. Or spend that 15 seconds ordering flowers on Tuesday afternoon (in anticipation of or, if out of town, in lieu of, date night).

- *Focus on gratitude.* Take the time to show appreciation to your partner. This may sound simple enough, but many people tend to overlook this important task. Everyone loves being appreciated, most of all by the people who matter. Showing appreciation regularly not only makes your spouse feel better about you, it creates a significant romantic boost to the relationship. Gratitude returns us to the very beginning, when we spent the time appreciating and adoring our partner. That's not only good for the recipient, it creates more love and passion in the giver. Whether you verbalize it by saying, "Thank you for all that you have done, my love," or treat your partner to a home cooked meal, you show that you appreciate your spouse. Even better, take a few seconds every day to look your spouse in the eye, thank them and tell them how much you love them. While women may find that this sort of thing comes naturally, for men it usually is anything but natural. So combine both points in this section: put in a daily reminder for the way home to remember, think about, and appreciate my wife, and to actually thank my wife when I get home. You'll be shocked by the buzz of energy that this can create between you.

Be supportive during life events. Intimacy means being on par with your partner emotionally. That means supporting her no matter what. Be it through sickness, financial difficulties, starting a new business, a death of someone important, or even something trivial like needing a ride to work, or suffering through a missed or unpleasant appointment, do all that you can to be supportive of your partner, irrespective of the details. Share the burden. It's the right thing to do and it creates more closeness, which feeds the freshness of the relationship.

Touch each other. What happened to that hug hello? The peck on the cheek goodbye? That moment of sitting on the couch holding hands? A goodnight cuddle? A short back rub or foot massage? None of those small but significant gestures requires a babysitter or any expenditures. Once again, intimacy extends beyond the bedroom walls, but it feeds back to the bedroom in powerful ways.

Go to bed together. One of the simplest ways to keep intimacy alive in the relationship is not surprisingly among the the most overlooked. In today's fast-paced world, where we are forced constantly to juggle bizarre work schedules, children, projects, and endless activities and chores, many couples fall into the habit of going to bed at different times. Sometimes, given differing natures or job logistics it's unavoidable; but often it just sort of falls by the wayside through neglect. This leads to an unnecessary and undesirable disconnect between the partners, in turn weakening the bonds of intimacy in general, and sexual activity specifically. If you simply cannot sync your schedules to go to bed at the same time, then at the very least make sure you hug or snuggle and above all put to rest any tension between the two of you leftover from the day. A simple, "I'm sorry, my love, and sweet dreams," should suffice and will reaffirm for your spouse that you care about him, keeping alive the emotional connect that will translate into more physical contact and ever more freshness over time.

C. COMMUNICATE!

When it comes to our all-important sexuality, communication is critical. Many couples find it very difficult if not downright painful to speak openly about their sexual life, whether by way of praise and gratitude, or through the expression of needs and wants. That lack of clarity and openness usually leads to misunderstood messages and frustrating experiences. Communicating freely with one another underlies a living and developing intimate relationship. In the beginning you'll probably have to force yourselves to do it, usually with one of you taking the lead. After a time you'll come to look forward to those communications as a central way to develop the depth and intensity of the experience. As much as possible, praise and thank your spouse for the ways they take care of and try to please you. That feedback and gratitude loop creates a powerful positive cycle.

In the event that sexual dysfunction occurs — and we'd define dysfunction broadly as either side feeling regularly unsatisfied in the bedroom — then therapy with a certified professional should be considered a viable option. And don't wait too long. Along with sexual frustration will come resentment and distrust, which can worm their way more deeply into our psyches. It's usually far easier to nip the problem in the bud, so to speak, rather than allowing the weeds of negative emotion to spread.

D. Protect your relationship

Perhaps no area of marriage needs more protection from outside influences than that of our intimate life. Yet few of us even recognize the danger. For anything I consider important, I don't just do positive things, I also build protective fences around it. At times that means taking extreme measures, usually in correlation to how precious the subject is.

Some examples:

When it comes to my health, I don't stop with diet and exercise; I also don't smoke. In my financial life, I spend blood and sweat making money; but then I take pains to make sure it's protected from loss. When we build or buy a home, we furnish it, but we also put locks on the doors and install an alarm system.

The same is true at the level of my emotional and physical connection to my spouse (which surely is more precious than all other assets). Here too we need to protect ourselves from seemingly innocent outsiders or outright intruders that pose a threat to our marital oneness.

The number of Americans who are expected to cheat on their spouses over the course of a marriage is at least a quarter, and as much as three quarters, depending on the source and on which cohort you're measuring. Almost any way you look at it, the number of faithful spouses isn't likely any larger than the unfaithful. Rather than trying to repair the fence after it's been breached, we're much better off keeping it intact. That means implementing two separate approaches:

- Protect and defend the attraction I have for my spouse. This will obviate the need or desire to find satisfaction outside the marriage.
- Limit my opportunities to cheat. Staying out of harm's way helps to forestall opportunistic cheating, the type experienced by otherwise loving spouses.

Be careful what you look at. It doesn't matter who you marry, how "hot" he or she is, or how sensual. First, because over time that heat will cool. As one rabbi we know once said: Marrying for looks is like buying a stock you know will go down. Second, no matter how pretty and sexy she is, there will always be someone prettier and sexier and more unattainable (and therefore more desirable on a purely physical level). Simply put, guard your eyes from pornographic or otherwise sexually stimulating images and materials. This isn't about medieval prudishness or moralizing, it's about preserving the fragile attraction you have for your spouse beyond that first twelve months we cited above where sexual passion peaks. The unreal images don't end with the simple attractiveness of the woman on the screen. It's her passion or submissiveness or assertiveness or adventurousness that she so unabashedly expresses in those sex scenes. Your wife can't compete with Jennifer, and trust me, you can't compete with Brad. But in effect, that's just what we inadvertently force our spouses to do. It's a losing battle. It erodes attraction, and it lets the steam out of the relationship, especially in the bedroom. That drives even young marriages into old age fast.

Limit social media to what's necessary. One of the most subtle but pernicious effects of social media is the way in which it locks us into our past relationships. Is it a good idea to stay linked to my old girlfriends? Is that more likely to nurture trust from my spouse, or jealousy and insecurity? And on a bad day, after a fight with my husband, will that friendly and handsome old boyfriend offer a healthy outlet to express my frustration, or a new source of danger to my marriage? Why take the risk?

Add to this what we described above as social comparison theory, in which I continually evaluate my own life in light of what I perceive to be the lives of others. In a world of social media, where participants constantly broadcast images of themselves looking and acting their best and most exciting, my spouse — who is sometimes, but not *always*, sexy, beautiful and exciting (sometimes he has the flu; once in awhile she's pregnant and throwing up all day) — once again cannot compete. The old flame, on the other hand, doesn't post *those* pictures, always looks good, and often makes me think of those carefree times and passions.

142 ❧ NOT A PARTNERSHIP

Once again, we're not Luddites. Social media provides valid and often critical access to people we need for social, cultural, or business purposes. The problem is that by failing to acknowledge the inherent dangers lurking alongside the more important connections, we fail to put up any boundaries whatsoever. The result? Too much exposure to too much beauty and fantasy at the expense of my spouse and our intimate life.

PILLAR #2:
Gratitude: Feel It & Show It!

LIFE IS GOOD

It's a simple calculation: gratitude makes life better. For you and for everyone around you. To the ingrate, life in general, and people in particular, present a constant flow of disappointing failures to meet expectations, one after another. The funny thing is, it has almost nothing to do with actual circumstances, but everything to do with the inner attitude towards all the things that come our way.

POOR LITTLE RICH GUY

Sometimes it reaches the point of pathology. When Tod was working on Wall Street, many times he saw investment bankers or analysts literally crying over their mistreatment — receiving a $3 million bonus when they felt entitled to $4 million (a crime!). And while there *is* a game that's important to play skillfully to make sure that you get compensated (which involves always appearing to be unhappy at the shabby treatment to which you've been subjugated), for the ungrateful person the feeling of being cheated was often quite real.

BACK TO THE SUBLIME

That's by way of the absurd. But closer to home, literally and figuratively, we see the same negative dynamic and character trait. My wife makes dinner every night, but just never makes the roast beef the way I like it. My husband takes care of me, but forgets to take the garbage out. She takes care of the kids and works full time, yes, but I can't stand that she sometimes doesn't offer me a drink when I get home. And on, and on, and on. Without gratitude, I only notice what's lacking, one disappointment after another. I always feel mistreated.

Even if she prepares the roast beef the way I like it, it usually doesn't help much. In our work with couples we have seen a fundamental and repetitive story play out that looks something like this: They're both working crazy hours as bankers, lawyers, consultants or programmers (or whatever). Neither has time to exercise or to chill out, so they're both running ragged, unable to really take care of themselves physically and emotionally. Chapter two starts between 6 and 9 P.M., with the arrival of one or both at home. Especially if there are kids involved, the next several hours bring the nightly stressors of dinner and dishes, cleaning up the house, laundry, reading to and bathing the kids. It's clear to an outsider: both are living heroic and giving lives, providing for the family, building a home, putting aside many personal needs and luxuries for the sake of each other and their kids. But for them, rather than appreciating each other's sacrifice and generosity, they are overwhelmed by the stress. He feels she doesn't admire him for his sacrifice. She never hears words of appreciation for her endless work. That leads to resentment and withdrawal. Left unchecked, this can descend to hatred.

With gratitude, life — and particularly marriage, and even very stressful professional and family life — can provide one amazing experience after another. She married me, with all my faults? What a generous person! He brings home Chinese once a week so I can put my feet up? What a guy! She called to see how I was feeling? So thoughtful! We were able to have kids — how amazing! We got through the week without a crisis...I have a job and we have food on the table...we get a little vacation here and there.... Life is *good*!

THE THANKS I GIVE!

According to research summarized by Harvard Medical School, "gratitude is strongly and consistently associated with greater happiness. Gratitude helps people feel more positive emotions, relish good experiences, improve their health, deal with adversity, and build strong relationships."[52]

Psychology Today,[53] citing numerous studies, finds that gratitude:

---

52. Harvard Mental Heath Letter. "In Praise of Gratitude." November, 2011, www.health.harvard.edu/newsletter_article/in-praise-of-gratitude.
53. Morin, Amy. "7 Scientifically Proven Benefits of Gratitude." *Psychology Today*. April 3, 2015, www.psychologytoday.com/us/blog/what-mentally-strong-people-dont-do/201504/7-scientifically-proven-benefits-gratitude.

1. ...opens the door to more relationships
2. ...improves physical health
3. ...improves psychological health
4. ...enhances empathy and reduces aggression
5. ...is associated with better sleep
6. ...improves self-esteem
7. ...increases mental strength

The grateful person is easy to please, always sees the good, is easy to love and makes others feel loved, and just has a way of picking up everyone around him or her.

No place like home

Beyond the power gratitude packs to improve life generally, it has particular dynamism in the home. According to researchers at the University of California, Berkeley, "[w]hereas existing research suggests that appreciation is particularly important in the formation of relationships...our research suggests that appreciation is beneficial for the health and maintenance of intimate romantic bonds...appreciation influences relationship maintenance in daily life, in dyadic interactions, and over the course of time. Our research suggests that Adam Smith was certainly on to something when he commented on the central importance of gratitude in our lives; cultivating appreciation may be just what we need to hold onto healthy, happy relationships that thrive."[54]

---

54. Gordon, Amie M., et al. "To Have and to Hold: Gratitude Promotes Relationship Maintenance in Intimate Bonds." *Journal of Personality and Social Psychology*. August, 2012, greatergood.berkeley.edu/images/application_uploads/gordon-RelationshipMaintenance_1.pdf.

Berkeley Wellness further reports that "researchers found that expressing and perceiving gratitude helps protect marriages from the adverse effects of conflicts. They interviewed 468 married people about the degree to which they felt appreciated by their spouse, their level of financial strain and the conflicts this caused, and their marriage quality. Spousal gratitude was found to be the best predictor of marital quality and seemed to have protective effects — that is, spouses who consistently perceived gratitude and appreciation from their partner were less likely to suffer the marital instability (as evidenced, for instance, by thoughts about divorce) that can result from marital stress and conflict. And there may be a positive 'spillover effect,' as people who feel appreciated by their spouse are more likely to express their gratitude, leading to a feedback loop (what goes around, comes around) of more positive behaviors and attitudes."[55]

ALL ABOUT ME

It's tempting to think of gratitude as something I do to benefit my spouse. That is for sure true, but it's only part of the picture. In fascinating research led by Sara Algoe at the University of North Carolina at Chapel Hill (as summarized in *Scientific American*[56]), "[e]xpressing gratitude on a regular basis can help you appreciate your partner rather than taking his or her small favors or kind acts for granted, and that boost in appreciation strengthens your relationship over time.... On days that people felt more gratitude toward

---

55. *Berkeley Wellness*. "The Benefits of Gratitude." November 19, 2015, www.berkeleywellness.com/healthy-mind/mood/article/benefits-gratitude.
56. Pawelski, Suzann P. "The Happy Couple." *Scientific American*. October 23, 2012, www.scientificamerican.com/article/the-happy-couple-2012-10-23.

their partner, they felt better about their relationship and more connected to him or her; they also experienced greater relationship satisfaction the following day. Additionally, their partners (the recipients of the gratitude) were more satisfied with the relationship and more connected to them on that same day. Thus, moments of gratitude may act as a booster shot for romantic relationships."

Algoe and her colleagues further found that the "participants' reported feelings of gratitude towards a romantic partner predicted who would stay in their relationships and who would break up nine months later. The more grateful participants were, the more likely they were to still be in their relationship."[57]

Come again? Yes, you heard right. The more gratitude I feel and express the happier, more fulfilled and more committed I myself will be in the relationship! That positivity and appreciation in turn kick-starts a deeper sense of well-being and security in my spouse, nurturing a reciprocal sense of gratitude towards me, which in turn fortifies me. It's hard to overstate the power of this ultimate virtuous cycle in the building of a profoundly happy marriage.

Once again, as in all arenas of giving, it's in my own hands. I can't — and needn't, and shouldn't — wait for my spouse. I have the power to create a deeper sense of satisfaction and contentment in myself and my spouse, as individuals and as a unified entity. What am I waiting for?

---

57. Gordon, Amie M. "Gratitude is For Lovers." *Greater Good Magazine*. February 5, 2013, greatergood.berkeley.edu/article/item/gratitude_is_for_lovers.

Have to admit

Clearly the word "thanks" means to show gratitude or appreciation. The word is thought to derive its roots from from the Old English thancas (plural of thanc), relating to the word "think," or to Proto-Germanic roots relating to thought/remembrance/gratitude[58] — as in giving thought and having gratitude for what you did for me.

In the language of the Bible, the roots go a bit deeper. The Hebrew word for "thanks" is *todah*. That word is based on a root structure that actually means "to admit." So in simple terms, saying *todah* checks the box of showing some appreciation for what the other gave to me. But at a more profound level, it expresses an admission: I need you; I couldn't have done it without you; I'm not self-sufficient; you helped complete me.

Perhaps that's why so many (especially male) spouses have a hard time saying it. It connotes a certain vulnerability, a little chink in the armor of total independence. It also builds trust, love, affection, confidence and well-being in the other, while at the same time fortifying the relationship.

How far does it go?

Jewish law and custom is filled with extreme examples of just how far we are meant to feel and express gratitude. In one of the most famous examples, amidst the meting out of the plagues in Egypt, Moses passes the baton, so to speak, to his brother Aaron when it comes to striking the Nile River with his staff to kick off the first two plagues of blood and lice. Why didn't Moses hit the water himself? Because

---

58. https://en.wiktionary.org/wiki/thank.

Moses felt it would be an act of ingratitude to strike that same Nile which hid him when he was a newborn and the Egyptians were killing all the Jewish male babies. Of course the Nile didn't know the difference, and that's not the point. Gratitude is not just something that the giver is owed and needs to see expressed; it's a fundamental attitude and sensitivity that I, as recipient, need to develop within myself at all times in all relationships.

Nor is this concept just an inspiring theory. Rabbi Yisroel Zev Gustman was a famous Talmudic scholar who spent the final three decades of life (until passing away in his 80s) as head of an advanced academy in Jerusalem. Some students noticed that this distinguished and famed rabbi used to go out daily to water the plants in the garden surrounding the building. Somewhat astonished, they asked him why he was doing such menial and time-consuming work. He explained to them that when he was a young man in Lithuania, fleeing for his life from the Nazis during the Holocaust, he survived on plants, and was at times hidden by them. Forever he felt a debt of gratitude to the plant world, and expressed it daily by giving back. It may have made little impression on the rose bushes, but it certainly made an indelible imprint on those students and all who have heard the story.

THE FIRST ACT OF INGRATITUDE

The opportunity to feel and express gratitude exists in all contexts and relationships. But nowhere — nowhere! — does it find a home that is more fitting than, well, the home. Marriage provides a constant forum for playing it out and making it real. Each of the hundreds of weekly encounters with my spouse, large and small, offers the opportunity to express my appreciation. It is no surprise, then, that mankind's first recorded act of ingratitude was exactly there.

Let's revisit Adam and Eve. Love, oneness, co-mingled souls, life in Eden. And then came the sin. She eats from the Tree of Knowledge of good and evil, and then she gives the fruit to him and he also eats. Shortly thereafter the following conversation ensues.

> The Lord God called out to the man and said to him, "Where are you?"
>
> He replied, "I heard the sound of You in the garden, and I was afraid because I was naked, so I hid."
>
> Then He asked, "Who told you that you were naked? Did you eat of the tree from which I had forbidden you to eat?"
>
> The man said, "The woman You put at my side — she gave me of the tree, and I ate."[59]

Ouch. Not the answer we were looking for. But the point is clear: that same spouse who initially I feel is flesh of my flesh, the one who completes me, supports me, takes care of me, loves me despite my shortcomings, the one whose beneficence towards me is, in truth, boundless — that's exactly the one I take for granted. Oh, and that the Creator bestowed her upon me as the ultimate gift and blessing, no big deal; she didn't meet expectations....

PENNY WISE

The failure to feel gratitude for a spouse doesn't necessarily

---
59. Genesis 3:9-12.

evince a fundamental inability in the thankless husband. To the contrary, do the slightest favor for him at work, hold the elevator door for him for 5 seconds, even just push the third-floor button and he will bestow gratitude upon you. "Thank you so much!"

And that time he left his credit card on the counter at the cafe, and the barista ran outside and gave it to him on the sidewalk, that's a story he told for days, even going as far as sending a special note to the manager citing the amazing act of human kindness.

Such expressions of thanks are appropriate, and at times border on the noble. So why are we so deficient when it comes to having the same presence of mind and same overwhelming feeling of appreciation when my wife runs out of the house with that document I forgot to take as I'm pulling out of the driveway? I'll probably say thank you in the moment, but I won't likely write a letter to my children citing the incredible act of giving I was subject to. Why not?

Entitlement system

We all enter the world as little kings and queens — bathed, swaddled, clothed, fed on demand. What constitutes a right for me — being taken care of — is at once a duty for the other. The more selfless and giving the parent, the more naturally entitled the child. Life of course is a long-term process of growth along the pathway from child to adult, from cared for to caring, from unaware to self-aware, from taking to giving. For many of us, however, that fundamental sense of entitlement never really goes away. By definition, if I'm entitled, I won't feel a sense of gratitude. I may check the box of saying thank you, since that shows good form, but it may be more affectation than affection.

The kid who grew up watching a critical or abusive mother or father constantly making demands upon the spouse may well have further inculcated negative and harmful feelings of what he or she is owed by a compliant spouse. The last thing I'll feel about something I'm owed is a feeling of gratitude.

Problem one, then, in developing gratitude, lies in the idea that I had it coming to me. In emotional terms, I'm still a child, however accomplished I may be in other spheres of life. Left unchecked, the ungrateful spouse can slowly corrupt and eat away at the underlying and unifying fabric of giving with which nearly every marriage starts. Simply put, it's really hard to keep giving to someone who never notices and never appreciates.

But that's only part of the story.

SMELL TEST

Do you remember the last time you walked into the cosmetics section of a fancy department store? The intoxicating cacophony of perfumes! Or how about a French bakery. *Ooh la la*, the overpowering smell of fresh pastries and out-of-the-oven breads! And do you remember what happened next? Well, if that cosmetic counter or patisserie was your place of work, you probably spent the entire day without noticing any smell at all past the first few minutes of arriving (and not beyond your first Danish if you were a customer). Why? Because we all suffer from (or benefit from, in case you work in a tannery or a gym...) something called olfactory fatigue, or olfactory adaptation, which is defined as "the temporary, normal inability to distinguish a particular odor after a prolonged exposure to that airborne compound."[60] After a period of time, we simply don't notice the odor, however aromatic it might be.

In much the same way, pervasive acts of kindness — the type we experience at the hands of our spouse at home, rather than, say, the episodic elevator door hold at work — go unnoticed. It's not that we don't understand their value and beauty, we simply don't see it. Perversely, the more kind and giving my spouse is, the harder it is to detect. The kindness of strangers, so unexpected, is like getting a smell of barbecued ribs while sitting in the patisserie. It's far easier to notice, enjoy and appreciate.

In a way, this second phenomenon — "receiving fatigue," if you will — is more difficult to self-correct. Even someone with good character, who genuinely tries to think of others, just doesn't notice the goodness that is poured into his or her life by the other. We're too habituated. To make matters worse, what *does* get noticed is literally anything that goes wrong or is not to his or her liking.

It's hard to overstate the perversity. It's precisely *because* my wife or husband so regularly, consistently and frequently gives to me that I don't notice. What *does* arouse my attention? Anything that's out of character. The more unexpected (and negative things from loving spouses are by definition unexpected), the more I notice it. I'm frustrated, disappointed, and sometimes quite angry.

---

60. https://en.wikipedia.org/wiki/Olfactory_fatigue.

Well done!

As part of an ancient Jewish custom, every Friday night before the Sabbath meal, the wife lights candles at the table. The sages describe this custom as bringing peace into the home. In simple terms, light means that we can see each other, won't trip over each other, knock into things. Thus we "keep the peace." But there's a much deeper idea that every spouse can integrate. Light creates a wider field of vision. The more light, the more context I have for each thing I look at. So, for example, when I see with limited vision, if my wife hands me a well-done piece of roast beef, and I love it rare, all I will see is the failure to deliver what I wanted. She didn't take the time, doesn't care enough, blew it again. When there's light, I can expand my field of vision. Whoa — surrounding that well-done piece of beef are the vegetables I love. And look how the silverware was polished and arranged, and what a beautiful cloth was spread on the table. And there's a basket of bread. And see how the room is sparkling! Without light, I hyperfocus on the single thing in front of me, blowing it totally out of proportion. Within a broader framework, it's a small flaw amidst a most positive and uplifting mosaic.

Our first goal, then, must involve learning to actually see and feel and appreciate the goodness my spouse brings to the table of our marriage. We'll address the "how" a bit further down.

Lethal combination

When we morph the two enemies of appreciation — entitlement and habituation (receiving fatigue) — into a single blurred reality, the results can turn lethal. With cruel irony, it's precisely my spouse, the one who gives the most to me and to whom I am most indebted, that I tend to victimize. In the words of one of the great masters of the human psyche of the 20th century, Rabbi Shlomo Wolbe: "The closer the relationship is between two people, the more difficult it is for them to recognize the goodness. So much do we become habituated to receiving kindness from one another that over the course of time we can tend to think that the other person is obligated in his kindness to us, and if on any given occasion he would diminish the kindness that he normally does, he will be held accountable for not having fulfilled his duty. This approach darkens our relationships — particularly with our families."[61]

What to do?

Gratitude mandates two distinct responses: *feeling* it and *expressing* it.

With respect to feeling gratitude: Good training can help us check the box of saying "Thank you," and "I appreciate what you did for me." The problem is that, especially in marriage, politeness will only get you so far. Your spouse knows the difference between heartfelt appreciation and good form.

In a classic work on non-verbal communication published in 1971, researcher Albert Mehrabian studied the

---
61. Rabbi Shlomo Wolbe, *Alei Shor*, vol. II, pp. 281-282.

sales process, ascribing weights to the various aspects that made up the dance between salesperson and potential customer. Mehrabian determined that "prospects based their assessments of credibility on factors other than the words the salesperson spoke — the prospects studied assigned 55 percent of their weight to the speaker's body language and another 38 percent to the tone and music of their voice. They assigned only 7 percent of their credibility assessment to the salesperson's actual words."[62] If that's true when you're buying a used car, how much more must it be so when dealing with your husband or wife?

To be sure, manners help, and a lack of manners can be catastrophic. But your spouse needs authenticity in your expression that he or she is appreciated. One genuine feeling can generate the manifold positives that gratitude can provide.

TALKING THE TALK

All of us know it to be true, but let's, well, say it: Feeling gratitude without expressing it doesn't cut it. It's like a farmer who grows an abundant crop of wheat and fails to harvest. Men classically have a more difficult time of it than women. Psychologists sometimes refer to it as "normative male alexithymia," a wildly non-intuitive phrase that "refers to the fact that traditional masculine role socialization channels many men into ways of being such that their masculine identity conflicts with many emotions they feel and what they feel they are 'allowed' to express (i.e., they will be shamed and

---

62. Yaffe, Philip. "The 7% Rule: Fact, Fiction, or Misunderstanding." *Ubiquity*. October 2011, ubiquity.acm.org/article.cfm?id=2043156.

will feel as if they are 'not real men' if they express feelings of vulnerability, dependency needs, weakness, etc.)."[63]

We're reminded of the old song in *Fiddler on the Roof* where the husband of 25 years, Tevye, squirms and just can't seem to respond to his wife Golde's simple question of "Do you love me?" While many women have no problem expressing their feelings, for men it produces a sort of trauma. Many men actually do feel a deep sense of gratitude for their wives, but simply can't bring themselves to say it. It makes them feel weak somehow. The problem is compounded when we believe that *feeling* gratitude (or love or admiration) suffices. It doesn't. To the contrary, there is no end to how much gratitude needs to be expressed verbally. It's true in all our relationships, but particularly in marriage.

Here's how Rabbi Wolbe sums it up: "Love that is not met with appreciation will not last. As great as the love may have been at the beginning, if, with the passage of time, one does not appreciate the goodness that the other bestows on him, their love will not last; it even stands to transform into hatred.... Such is the case in all relationships: children and their parents, partners and friends at work, and a manager and his employees. It is best that the training in this case be connected with concrete action.... One needs to actually express his gratitude verbally and not just keep it in his heart."[64]

---

63. Henriques, Gregg. "Why Is It So Hard for Some Men to Share Their Feelings?" *Psychology Today*. November 13, 2014, www.psychologytoday.com/us/blog/theory-knowledge/201411/why-is-it-so-hard-some-men-share-their-feelings.
64. Rabbi Shlomo Wolbe, *Alei Shor*, vol. II, p. 279.

FAILED ATTEMPTS

Not only must we say it, we must say it right. Every husband and wife needs to express gratitude which 1) feels authentic and real to the person who is expressing it, and 2) is expressed in a way that the person on the receiving end needs to hear it. For example, a shy person may be embarrassed by public signs of gratitude, such as announcements in front of other people. If he's angry or distracted at the time she says thank you for an appreciated gesture, the expression may go unnoticed or even provoke a negative response. Bad timing or inappropriate context can cause a misfire despite the love and authenticity that went into the expression.

PRACTICAL STEPS: PRACTICE MAKES PERFECT

Got it. It's tough. First I have to train myself to feel it. Then I have to learn to say it. Where and how do I begin?

Back to Google: 94 million results on how to feel gratitude, and 68 million on how to express it. Done! If only we knew where to begin.

The Jewish sources on personal character development teach us that character change always involves four steps:

1. Look at yourself honestly; take an accounting. Determine where you need work. Pick one particular area where you come up short.
2. Think deeply and do research until you build a clear picture of how you'd like to develop yourself, where you want to go, what you want to express.

3. Start practicing it (whatever the "it" is that you'd like to make part of your life). Practice it over and over and over and over again, until the bad trait is overcome and the good trait develops internally and organically and becomes part of your makeup.
4. Pull back and utilize the good trait in a balanced and healthy way.

Til your face turns blue

Let's take a simple, related, and important example.

Step one: Take a hard look at yourself and determine the most important aspect of yourself that you would like to change. If you have any trouble coming up with something, just ask your wife. Let's say your conclusion is that you are stingy. What's next?

Step two: Think as deeply as possible about why the inability to give to others destroys relationships, and about the beauty and power and nobility of sharing your blessings. Consider what you'd like your child to say about you at your funeral ("She was totally giving to others!"). Read the first 10 articles on Google about the destruction caused by stinginess and the power of generosity. Think about people you truly respect and look up to; chances are high that they are charitable, generous.

Step three: Just do it. Start putting your hand into your pocket and giving to the needy, whether you deem them fully worthy or not. Start writing checks. Offer extra help to those around you. Spend more on those birthday and anniversary presents. If you're (also) stingy with yourself, start splurging on your own well-being; live it up! In short, go overboard, and keep going overboard, beyond what a balanced and thoughtful giver would view as responsible and appropriate. In doing so, you'll eventually both break the bad trait of stinginess and open up a new reservoir of natural generosity that will begin to overflow your own banks naturally, spilling over to others.

Step four: Go back to step one and measure how you're doing. Assuming you've actually begun to truly build generosity into your core character, you can now begin to pull back to a normal, healthy and balanced approach. Then make sure, and this is critical, that you spend time periodically measuring your progress to make sure that you aren't backsliding. Put it into your calendar, just like Ben Franklin did in his day, to objectively and dispassionately see how you're doing. Franklin worked on 13 virtues in order, spending a week on each in a constantly repeating cycle. That meant coming upon each objective four times a year for a week each. We're suggesting only one at a time, but at the very least a monthly personal accounting — certainly nothing less than you'd do for your checking account — to make sure you're still in the black. If you are, go on to the next internal fixer-upper project.

The Gratitude Plan

Let's assume that based upon the foregoing you've accomplished Steps 1 & 2. You're now convinced that:

1. Gratitude is mission critical
2. You're not very good at feeling or expressing it
3. You are now going to change all that.

Let's develop the plan.

Backhands and Compliments

Here's the good news for the strong silent types and you super introverts: You needn't be an articulate, eloquent and loquacious speaker to express gratitude. There is no right and wrong when it comes to the words or actions you choose. And here's the not so good news: Whatever you do say — and you need to say it a lot — must be said in a *genuine* manner, and it should take into account the type of appreciation your spouse needs to hear, see or feel (this is where a book like *The Five Love Languages* can be particularly useful, as one spouse needs words of affirmation, another needs physical touch, etc.).

If you're not exactly sure how your spouse most wants your thanks, just ask! Above all, never make the classic mistake of assuming your spouse naturally intuits how much you appreciate him or her. You have to express it.

As we noted above in the stingy-to-generous process, when it comes to developing a new good habit, or ridding yourself of the negative, it all begins with repetition. Lots of it, and for a long time. A budding tennis player will hit thousands of backhands before they become second nature.

The pro will also practice all day long, in and out of season, focusing on greater nuance or power or form. It's no different when it comes to expressing gratitude. Start doing it now, and go way overboard until it becomes natural.

Strategy #1: Express it

1. *Involve your smartphone.*

Start by creating some recurring calendar items. Time your first one to come along with your alarm ("Tell him how amazing she/he is before leaving the house"). Schedule another one for the afternoon ("No matter how busy and preoccupied I am, write her a note of thanks and love"), and another one for coming-home time ("Don't forget, no matter how hard my day was, to show gratitude this evening"). Try a final one around bedtime ("Tell her how lucky I am to be married to her"). Don't worry that he knows that you're being prompted. You can use the humor to your advantage ("My iPhone just reminded me to remind myself how amazing you are!"). Moreover, she'll be amazed by the effort since it's for her. By the time it begins to become tiresome, the expressions will have become more spontaneous and natural. At that point, leave the reminders in your calendar anyway, since habituation tends to creep back in when you least expect it.

2. *Don't wait for dramatic acts of kindness to say thank you.*

Thank your spouse for the little things, the cup of water, the smile or hug or words of affirmation when you needed it, for the dinner, the cleaning, the laundry, for picking up the groceries, for letting you sleep an extra half hour on the weekend. Say it and say it again.

3. Use body language.

Ten words of thanks while you're walking away or simultaneously looking at your smartphone can't compare to two words with clear eye contact. If he likes affection, say it with a hug or peck on the cheek. Show that the words are coming from all of you, not just from some check the box portion of your brain that signalled your mouth (though that is still better than nothing).

4. Change it up.

Be creative. Use different words and ways of expressing your gratitude. Saying nothing but "thank you" all the time loses its meaning after a while. Make your language more colorful: "It really means a lot to me when you...," "I appreciate that you...," "I am so grateful for...."

5. Don't forget the classics.

Again, put the reminders in your calendar. "Bring home flowers every Friday evening." "Leave a little box of chocolates." Above all, don't forget to attach the slightest little note: "Because you are the best," "Thanks for giving me a great week," "You're always there for me."

6. Write it down.

Let's spend a bit more time on one last practical exercise, "The Gratitude Letter." In a 2005 study, Martin Seligman, founder of the Positive Psychology Center at the University of Pennsylvania, found that of five major strategies tested, it was specifically the writing of a thoughtful and detailed letter that most powerfully increased feelings of gratitude in the writer, while at the same time making the recipient feel appreciated and valued. Beyond the immediate impact, the gratitude letter also "had the greatest positive impact on happiness one month later. Those who delivered and read the letter to the recipient in person, rather than just mailing it, reaped the greatest benefits."[65]

We suggest you focus the Gratitude Letter on your spouse's birthday and on your anniversary. Of course you have to buy the present, but spend most of your time on the note that you attach that expresses your love and gratitude. Brainstorm ways that he or she has contributed to you, and had positive effects on your life. Try to include both general and specific things this person has done for you and how his or her actions have made you feel. Find that great moment with your spouse, give the present, and read the note aloud. Remember: Babies push aside the gift and play with the box; little kids throw away the card and go for the toy; your spouse will keep the card long after the gift has been lost, gone out of style or been broken.

But make no mistake, even such powerful and love-affirming expressions have a shelf life. Seligman found that "six months after writing and delivering their Gratitude Letter, participants' happiness levels had dropped back down to where they were before the visit. This finding reminds us that no single activity is a panacea that can permanently alter happiness levels after just one attempt.

---

65. Breines, Juliana. "Four Great Gratitude Strategies." *Greater Good Magazine.* June 30, 2015, greatergood.berkeley.edu/article/item/four_great_gratitude_strategies.

Instead, gratitude practices and other happiness-inducing activities need to be practiced regularly over time, ideally with some variety to avoid hedonic adaptation."[66]

Strategy #2: Feel it

As you develop your frequency and consistency in expressing gratitude, you will naturally begin to feel it. However, don't leave it at that. We need to focus special attention on developing and fostering our internal appreciation as well.

One of the most powerful tools we've encountered for developing the feeling of gratitude is known as the "Three Blessings Exercise," sort of a handy implementation of the old maxim of "count your blessings." According to researchers at the University of California, Berkeley, the exercise "involves spending 5 to 10 minutes at the end of each day writing in detail about three things that went well that day, large or small, and also describing why you think they happened. In his 2005 study, Martin Seligman found that completing this exercise every day for one week led to increases in happiness that persisted for six months.

"This simple practice is effective because it not only helps you remember and appreciate good things that happened in the past; it can also teach you to notice and savor positive events as they happen in the moment, and remember them more vividly later on. By reflecting on the sources of these good things, the idea is that you start to see a broader ecosystem of goodness around you rather than assuming that the universe is conspiring against you."[67]

---

66. Breines, J.
67. Breines, J.

Seligman further found that the Three Blessings strategy compares favorably to antidepressant medication and psychotherapy. Moreover, while the exercise originally developed as a tool to develop gratitude generally, our experience has shown us that this exercise can be channeled directly towards marriage. The nightly questions become: What 3 things has my spouse done for me today? Don't think about the big picture; focus on small, practical and directed things that happened throughout the day, the sort of non-dramatic but life-enriching things that either I've come to expect as natural or that I'd otherwise overlook. She called to see how my meeting went. She gave me space to chill out when I got home. She made the salad I love for dinner. She made the bed. She took out the garbage. You'll likely find there is almost no end to all the acts of kindness she does directly or indirectly for my benefit or enjoyment.

If you can get your schedules in sync, you can also practice the Three Blessings exercise together by creating a shared gratitude journal. Not only will your awareness of her kindness grow, so will her awareness of your awareness, and vice-versa. Try it for a two-week period. Besides creating a more powerful atmosphere of positive energy, the two of you will very likely drive a new and more powerful phase of giving. Most of us, when noticed and positively reinforced by the recipient of our kindness, will naturally tend to do more and more. This is a great way to kickstart the amazing cycle of reciprocity that gratitude generates. Once that happens, everything begins to improve, from intimacy to the overall air of tranquility and happiness in the home.

PILLAR #3:
Respect in All Its Forms

When it comes to identifying the key ingredient in a successful marriage, many of us instinctively assume that it is love. Certainly in Western culture, we look to love to provide the intoxicating, if elusive and often short-lived, goal of happiness and fulfillment with our partner. The problem begins when we mistake romance for love, and we fool ourselves into believing it will last. Romance is by nature a critical but temporary state of euphoria that helps us get involved in a relationship. We inevitably face disappointment — often over and over again — if we don't ultimately evolve the relationship from that short-term high to the longer-lasting mode of giving and devotion that more appropriately defines and constitutes real love. Unfortunately, we generally fail in that department because the transition doesn't happen naturally. The bridge that is meant to connect us from the dramatic and exhilarating place of romance to the calm and tranquil shores of love and giving always seems a bit too short.

How can a couple ever hope to cross that divide? The answer is: through respect in all its forms. When we show our spouse that we honor and respect him or her, through speech and action and spending and overall behavior, it naturally leads to and helps to sustain real love.

Know it when I feel it

Respect is one of those elusive terms that are very difficult to define. Being treated nicely? Feeling that we're admired? Receiving deferential service? Kind speech? We certainly sense it when it's missing. Just think of a disrespectful husband or wife, or a rude kid. But what exactly is it?

Common definitions usually include phrases like "to hold in esteem" or "to admire." Once again let's turn to classical Hebrew, where the word for respect is *"kavod."* *Kavod* is itself an odd word because it shares a common root with the word *"kaved,"* which means heavy or weighty. It's not by accident; each sheds light on the other. Putting the two ideas together, respect is more aptly described as giving weight to the other person. If I view the other as weighty, I'll walk around him, give him precedence, think carefully about how I speak and act towards him. It is made up of both an attitude regarding the absolute importance and centrality of the other person in my life, and the million and one details of speech and actions that bring it to life.

Imagine the following: Your boss calls and says she'd like to see you. Unlikely you'll answer, "Yes, I should be free in five minutes, so please come down to my office and I'll make some time for you." Well, not if you plan to keep your job. The reason? Your boss is the "heavy" in the relationship. You walk around her, you think constantly about how she will feel or react.

And just how would I act around my boss, or in fact around anyone who is entitled to or deserving of my respect? How about if the Governor were coming for a visit? My speech will be pleasant, my demeanor calm, my attitude positive. I'll say please and thank you and go out of my way to show thoughtfulness and kindness. I'll rush to hold the door. It's likely that I'll be nothing short of clever, creative and enthusiastic in thinking of ways to make a good impression, to help out, to go the extra mile. The way I look, speak and act, including my body language and eye contact, will reflect an overall desire to please, and will make it clear who comes first. Above all, never, ever will I be rude or impatient or demanding or fail to say please or drop my guard.

Well, if that's the way it is with someone who may not care much for you, gives little thought to how to make your life better, doesn't carry you in her heart at all times, is anything but devoted to you and your well-being, and may in fact be quite a low-life in many personal matters — just how is it that so little of that amazing, careful and thoughtful behavior gets transfered to my wife?

WHEN OUR LOVE WAS NEW...

In case you'd like to take the self-test for how you are doing in the giving respect department, just ask yourself the following (painful) questions about how you've changed since the dating period until now:

- How careful were you to make an effort to look your best at all times? How about now?
- How much thought went into how you dressed, how you *smelled*?
- Did you ever ignore your date by texting while you were together?
- Was your speech more controlled, more loving, more respectful, more dignified?
- How were your manners and care for how you were perceived by the other? Did you open the door for her? Did you smile and praise and thank him for the smallest gesture?

All an act

We know the defense: there was a lot of acting there! I had to give my best performance in the beginning to get her interested! But this is real life, and we're married and love each other and home is the one place I never have to pretend.

Well, guess what? We still need to act throughout our married and parental lives. In fact, when it comes to our most important relationships, too much "authenticity" can be destructive if not lethal. Let's take an obvious example. A mother comes home from a tough day at work, exhausted. Everything went wrong today. She's *not* in a good mood. Most of the way home she scowls. All she wants is some peace and quiet, a quick dinner, some time on a friendly electronic device, and bed. As she enters the house, she's greeted by her three-year-old son who can't wait to show her his collection of today's finger paintings, in which all but 6% was done outside the lines of the images, and all with one color. At that moment Mom has a choice: authenticity or acting. Should she be "authentic" and abandon the child to the arbitrariness of today's mood, or, to the contrary, get out of her present self to be the mother her son needs right now? Obviously, any mother (or father) worthy of the title will break out into a huge smile at that moment and tell the little chap that she thought of nothing all day but the time she'd get to spend looking at his marvelous artworks. That way she builds the child and her relationship with him, rather than disappointing (and perhaps breaking) him and widening the parent-child gap between them.

Sometimes I need to put on an act, because the act is what the real me is supposed to be.

STILL THE ONE

Needless to say, you've already got the point that the same applies to your spouse. Before she can hear about your horrible day, she needs reassurance that she's not the problem, that you're happy to see her, that you respect and love her. He needs to know that however frustrating work was, or the kids were, you still can't wait to be in his arms, that you still look up to him. That "act" gives the other the feeling that *they* are the most important thing in your life, and not your boss, or colleague, or client or patient. That feeling of mattering in turn produces the sense of well-being that will enable the other to open up to hearing about and absorbing your problems and pains and frustrations.

The paradigm shift is that the act is really the deeper version of authenticity. What's false is the notion that because my boss yelled at me I should be angry at or short-tempered with my wife, I don't have time for her, I can't listen to her or empathize with what she might have faced today.

Our acting during the dating process qualified for an Oscar. Why was I able to put on such a good act then, and not let my frustrations and stress dictate my demeanor? It was because I sensed the need and desire to show my best self. Who cared if I was tired or if things went badly that day? I looked great, spoke with dignity and listened carefully.

Moreover, all I thought about were his needs and wants. Intimacy was powerful and frequent. We stole time to speak with each other, to be with each other, to make each other feel special and cherished.

Clearly nowhere is that behavior more needed — and more lacking — than when it comes to how I treat my spouse *now*, as the marriage matures. Now he needs my support and encouragement more than ever. She craves my attention and needs to know she's the center of my concern, even as (or especially because) I spend most of the day with other people and other projects.

BEYOND ME

Before you cry out that it's just too much, again ask yourself this question: Do I show my true and authentic feelings of the moment to my boss and colleagues and clients? Or, to the contrary, do I act (and dress and groom and speak) in the way that *they* need me to act? And all that for the people who are *not* the center of my life. So with my spouse it's a case of "all the more so."

The moral of the story? Act like you did when you were

dating. That's the mindset and part of the strategy for keeping marriage fresh.

STALE-MATE

Just where did that initial respect go? Well, part of it dissipated as we began letting our guard down and taking our spouse for granted. The law of entropy applies to marriage just as it applies to thermodynamics. Like everything else which slides towards a state of chaos when left unchecked and uninvested-in, so goes the treatment of my spouse. Fresh turns to stale, and men and women begin making their classic mistakes of disrespect, often with good but misguided intentions.

It has been decades since psychologist Carol Gilligan began publishing groundbreaking work on gender differences,[68] and John Gray published his monumental book, *Men are from Mars, Women are from Venus*.[69] Those works popularized some of the primary ways in which men and women differ and why they often miss each other:

- Women like to talk to share problems while men can't listen without offering solutions.
- Men measure commitment via significant and dramatic acts while women keep score of many small actions.
- Women love to relate while men need to retreat to the cave on a regular basis, especially after a stressful day.

---

68. Gilligan, Carol. *In a Different Voice: Psychological Theory and Women's Development*. Harvard University Press, 1982.
69. John Gray, *Men are from Mars, Women are from Venus*. HarperCollins, 1992.

Despite our awareness of them, these variations in nature and sensitivity differences continue to cause no end of strife in marriages. Men continue to solve their wives' problems. Women continue to resent trips to the cave. Why? Isn't enlightenment enough? The answer is a resounding no, unless that awareness is translated into action via respect.

Getting out more

Marriage is a living laboratory for working on one's character. The process of character development requires getting out of yourself and into the other. Nowhere is that more relevant than when it comes to appreciating and responding to my spouse's needs, especially when they differ from my own. The reason a man must focus on listening to his wife's recap of the day's frustrating events each evening is not because he is interested (he's not), but because it's important to her. Never ever will she look forward to his coming home and rushing past her to whatever space he has defined as his sacred cave; but because it's a fundamental need, she must learn to respect it. That's how I show that you matter to me, that you are the heavy in the relationship.

At the same time, each of us needs to realize that as we play out our own needs (her litany, his cave) we are by no means relieved of all responsibility. To the contrary, she needs to create an awareness that too much listening will reach a tipping point where his dutiful and respectful absorption of her sharing will turn to frustration. And he, before the nightly retreat, must always set expectations: "My dear, I can't wait to sit with you and hear about your day; just please give me 30 minutes to calm down and pull myself together from a really stressful day." To leave her waiting, not knowing what happened or when and if you'll re-emerge, and unable to share her own day and feelings, is akin to cruelty and portrays a fundamental lack of respect. We can't overstate this point: Each encounter, something as simple as his or her coming home from work, is an opportunity to show the other that they matter, that we'll make space for them and respect their needs and sensitivities.

JOB ONE

The respect mindset focuses continually on the fact that your spouse needs you to have her in mind, that she is your first and most important connection outside yourself. Your husband craves admiration in the way you look at and speak to him. She needs to know and to be told and shown that he loves her, that she always resides at the center of his concern, and however busy and preoccupied he may be with his next project, she remains the single most important thing in his life.

The Jewish sages tell us that a man can make his wife glow through proper treatment, and that, on the other hand, upsetting his wife and making her cry is a very serious offense. By the same token, a woman has the power to take a nobody and turn him into a king, or take a king and turn him into a nobody. The operative variable? Respect.

RESPECTFULLY YOURS

Before a young man and woman enter into marriage in observant Jewish communities, they study the ins and outs of marriage, beginning with the mindsets and modes of behavior that will generate a happy, lasting and fulfilling relationship. Maimonides summarized millenia of Jewish mystical and practical teachings on the subject with concise instructions for both men and women.

For men, Maimonides writes: "Our sages commanded that a man honor his wife more than himself, and love her as he loves himself. If he has financial resources, he should spend for her benefit in accordance with his resources. He should not cast a superfluous measure of fear over her. He should talk with her gently, and be neither sad nor angry."[70]

For women: "And similarly, they commanded a woman to honor her husband exceedingly and to be in awe of him. She should carry out all her deeds according to his directives, considering him to be a prince or a king. She should follow the desires of his heart and shun everything that he disdains."[71]

Note that these precepts are universal. Second, note the premise that the needs of *the other* are paramount in determining how I act. Third, note that this 12th-century scholar is telling us that men and women are different and have different needs (although, as we mentioned earlier, not all men function in the "male" mode, nor do all women function in "female" mode; these are paradigms or archetypes). Finally, take a moment to think about how you would feel, how you would flourish, if your spouse treated you this way. How would you feel if they treated you this way *all the time*?

But make no mistake. My focus has to be on my responsibilities, not on my rights. Maimonides speaks to each

---

70. Maimonides, *Laws of Marriage*, chapter 15, paragraph 19.
71. Ibid., paragraph 20.

spouse only about obligations. That singular focus is the secret sauce that makes happy marriage possible. The moment I focus on what I'm due, two corrosive outcomes are inevitable: 1) I give up all responsibility and free will in making my marriage great, and 2) I set myself up for a lifetime of resentment and disappointment.

Happy marriage begins and ends when I take the initiative and make it happen, irrespective of what my spouse may or may not be putting in. The good news is that — aside from extremely dysfunctional spouses — a husband or wife who is properly and respectfully treated in this manner will tend to reciprocate. The ultimate virtuous cycle.

INSIDE (AND) OUT

Many responsible husbands and wives have a sense that job number one is to take care of their better half. The challenge is how to implement that job. Where do I begin? Do I address her inner world and focus on her spiritual needs, or do we begin with her physical side? And where exactly do his emotional needs fit in? Are they spiritual or physical — or do they straddle both ends of his being? There are so many parts to him or her!

Let's try to divide the work into its primary components.

Spiritual/emotional

The respect I have for my spouse's spiritual/emotional side is reflected primarily in how I speak to him or her. Respectful speech is defined partly as loving, soothing, unhurried, caring and respectful in tone. The other half of speech, or rather, communication, is made up of listening with interest, attention, eye contact and patience, whether to a shared experience, a frustration, a complaint, a request or any of the other manifold ways my spouse needs me to absorb and respond. The violations occur when I criticize or make fun of or speak coarsely or roughly in response to her communication to me, as well as when I fail to pay attention, when I try to solve her problems when she only needs to be heard and understood, and when I listen on my own terms rather than fulfilling the specific need of the other at that moment.

Physical

The physical side of my spouse is divided into two primary parts: intimacy and respect for physical well-being. We've already dealt with intimacy in Pillar #1. The respect component is how I protect and treasure and give precedence to the physical needs of my spouse, including how I spend money on and prioritize his or her needs. Respect happens when I consciously focus on generosity and thoughtfulness, and avoid stinginess and self-centeredness. Respect also happens when I protect and provide for my spouse's physical well-being.

ONE TRICK PONIES

While many women are able to successfully fulfill the various needs of their husbands, men tend to be superheros in one area and delinquent in others, often failing to realize that their wife's needs are broad. Thus we find the husband who generously spends on his wife, the sky's the limit, yet he doesn't speak with the type of respect that she needs (think: captain of industry type, used to having his way, dictatorial). Then there's the sensitive husband who always speaks with his wife with deference and decency, yet he doesn't realize that he has to be generous monetarily towards her. A well-meaning man can often fail to understand the importance that his wife attaches to looking put-together in public, that she needs access to the clothing, jewelry and accessories not as some type of materialistic obsession but as the essential way she expresses herself in the world. She also needs the freedom to spend appropriately on the family, and she needs him to understand that being constrained, forced to consult with him or having to ask him for money is humiliating. There is the husband who takes care of his wife's intimate needs but doesn't properly take her emotional needs into account.

Respect begins with the recognition that my spouse is a complex molecule of interlocking physical, emotional and spiritual needs and desires, and that my job is to nurture him or her and to fulfill those needs to the best of my ability.

You first

Couples often make a mistake in their prioritization of the people around them. You and your spouse come first, before everyone else — before the parents, before the in-laws, and even before the children. The tendency to prioritize the needs of children is rooted in the unshakable reality that they are vulnerable and can't yet take care of themselves. Nevertheless, once the basic physical and emotional needs of kids are met, the priority of each spouse has to be the other. Focusing on the kids while ignoring your spouse is one of the roads to hell that is paved with good intentions.

Our experience in counseling couples has shown that the greatest thing you can do to nurture happy and healthy children is build a loving, warm and happy relationship between you and your spouse. All else being equal, happy homes produce happy kids. Ignoring your spouse's needs (for attention, love, intimacy) for the sake of the kids ultimately backfires. Unhappy marriages — characterized by coldness at best and fighting at worst — make for unhealthy environments. Such surroundings often cause confused, agitated and insecure children, despite the attention you lavish upon them.

COMMUNICATION BREAKDOWN (AND BUILD-UP)

The more my spouse and I feel respected by each other, the more open and effective is our communication. When I don't feel respected, my confidence wanes. I feel small. I shut down. As Dr. Amy Bellows puts it: "Communication is the mortar that holds a relationship together – if it breaks down, the relationship will crumble. When spouses no longer communicate, a marriage nurtures no one. It is no longer a marriage. True communication involves respect for the other person as well as active energy on your part. These two skills are essential ingredients to making a relationship work."[72]

Here's how Bellows explains the dynamic:

> "We often immediately reject another's perceptions, especially when our views differ. This rejection may even be unconscious. We find ourselves ready to dispute the things our spouse has to say,

---

72. Bellows, Amy. "Good Communication in Marriage Starts with Respect." *Psych Central.* July 17, 2016, psychcentral.com/lib/good-communication-in-marriage-starts-with-respect.

to challenge them, or to hear them as threats. Obviously, such an attitude interferes with two-way communication. The first step to improved dialogues is to respect your partner. Respect allows you to accept another person's point of view whole-heartedly. Consider and value your spouse's perspectives or suggestions. Let your partner know that your respect and value for him or her supersedes the specific issue you are discussing."[73]

While we'll include a number of practical areas for work on respect below, it's worth reading Bellows' specific suggestions for how to improve communication. They include:

- 🐦 Take full responsibility for the dialogue.
- 🐦 Put your energy into the exchange.
- 🐦 Make a commitment to seeing the process through.
- 🐦 Express your thoughts and feelings fully and encourage your partner to do the same.
- 🐦 Resolve misunderstandings by asking questions and seeking clarifications rather than by getting angry.[74]

Respect leads to greater communication, and that in turn leads to a stronger foundation for the relationship, propelling us forward in good times and providing an anchor and ballast when the seas are rough.

---

73. Bellows, A.
74. Bellows, A.

CRITICAL MASS

One of the great no-nos of marriage, and one we are all guilty of, is criticism. Both for him and for her, frequent criticism introduces a sort of cancer into the soul that, when unchecked, can destroy my spouse's emotional health and ultimately the marriage itself.

Often the "helpful hints and comments" (at least that's how they're intended) come from a good place, especially when they come from a woman. How so? Many wives see the great potential their husbands hold, what he could accomplish and who he could be if he'd only unlock it. That's why she married him. She saw all that latent energy and capacity. Over time she comes to realize, though, that he's just not making it happen. If only he'd try harder, speak more nicely, watch what he eats, exercise more, show a bit more ambition. So, she begins to suggest, and then to request and then to demand, and then to outright criticize. The problem is that no man can handle criticism from his wife. Part of it is childishness, and part of it lies deeply rooted in his need to be looked up to by his wife, to be seen as wonderful and invincible. Each critique drives home the point that he is just not so.

Their own antipathy to criticism by no means precludes men from criticizing their wives. Male criticism, unlike the female variety, often springs from less noble sources. His criticism comes less from seeing her greatness and wanting to bring it to life and more from his character flaws, impulsiveness and selfishness. If the world revolves around me, then I like things to be done my way. Period. She steps out of line in the way she speaks or thinks or cooks or makes decisions regarding the kids or home furnishings, and he'll let her know, sometimes in the harshest terms.

Just as he gets wounded in his way by her criticism, she gets hurt in her way by his criticism. For the ego-driven male, getting married adds another source of respect and adoration in his life. He's got his buddies, boss, colleagues, parents and siblings — now he gets married and adds a new and important cheerleader to his team. If she criticizes him rather than inspiring him to the greatness she wishes to bring out, it backfires and wounds his pride, causing him to shut down and retreat. In a nutshell, no man was ever criticized to greatness. To the contrary, wounding an ego ultimately causes it to run away.

For a woman, it's a bit more subtle. Marriage doesn't so much add a source of respect and honor; rather, it replaces the ones that existed hitherto. A woman may tend to find her sense of worth and affirmation through her husband's feelings towards her. When he fails to provide her with a sense of worth, or worse, he replaces the positive regard which she so desires and cherishes with criticism, her sense of well-being begins to unravel at the core no matter how many others in her life praise her and affirm. Harsh and frequent criticism can ultimately undermine her sense of self-worth and confidence. We have seen put-together, intelligent and highly competent women reduced to insecure by unchecked verbal criticism over time.

BUILD IT AND THEY WILL COME

Criticism has to be replaced with praise and positivity. Coco Chanel once quipped that "as long as you know men are like children, you know everything." There happens to be a lot of truth in that. Inside that strong, confident, seemingly mature fellow is a little kid who loves to play and who craves attention and adulation. There's really no limit to the amount of praise a man can and needs to hear from his wife. But rather than write it off as ego and immaturity, or worse, fight it, a smart and respectful wife learns how to build her husband through his inner reality. Show a man you think he's great, and he'll strive for greatness. Show him that he's generous, and he'll act with generosity. Show him that he makes you feel so special because he's loving and warm, and he'll work tirelessly to develop that side of himself. Why? Because men hate to disappoint their wives. They long to be the hero. The extent to which a woman keeps telling him how amazing he is, he'll become that amazing. His ego gets co-opted into the process. He feels like a hero when he performs and gets noticed. That's the power a woman wields over the nature of a man.

For women, praise plays less to the ego and more to the need to feel loved and cherished, which can serve as the greatest driver of well-being. That sense of happiness and security that he can help nurture in her by placing her at the center of his concern and frequently letting her know spills over into all aspects of her richly emotional world. When a man shows his wife he trusts her judgement, looks up to her, thinks the world of her, he builds her. One young man we know with a spectacularly competent, upbeat, proactive and happy wife, told us the following:

"My wife was raised in a somewhat wealthy and sheltered environment in which most things were done for her. She was well educated but never had to take on a lot of responsibility either in the house or out of the house. When we got married, she was sort of insecure and would ask me my opinion about everything, and truthfully I wasn't sure how much I could rely on her judgment. Pretty early on I realized that I was at a crossroads. I could either spend my life looking over her shoulder on decisions about the kids and the house and spending and everything else, or I could empower her and show her I really trust her and am here for her when she needs me. Once I did that she developed the confidence to handle everything."

Positivity, encouragement and trust are the tools a man can use to help build his wife, while endless (really, endless) praise are the means by which a woman can bring out greatness in her husband.

Choose your battles!

Wait a minute! How about things that really need to be changed or that truly bother me or that I feel are important? I can never criticize my spouse? That can't be what you're suggesting! And it isn't. In fact pretty much everything that needs to be spoken in a marriage can be spoken about. But context, timing and style will determine whether it produces positive or negative outcomes.

Context

At its worst, too frequent criticism tears the other down. At its best it gets tuned out and ignored. And it often does both. In order for a specific negative comment to be received in a way that can lead to change, the general context of your marriage should be established as one of praise and positive reinforcement. Sandwiching criticism amidst words of affirmation will allow it to penetrate the listener without a backlash.

In their groundbreaking work with couples, researchers John Gottman and Robert Levenson found that "the difference between happy and unhappy couples is the balance between positive and negative interactions during conflict. There is a very specific ratio that makes love last. That 'magic ratio' is 5 to 1. This means that for every negative interaction during conflict, a stable and happy marriage has five (or more) positive interactions.... On the other hand, unhappy couples tend to engage in fewer positive interactions to compensate for their escalating negativity. If the positive-to-negative ratio during conflict is 1-to-1 or less, that's unhealthy, and indicates a couple teetering on the edge of divorce."[75]

Respect, in all its forms, creates the overall backdrop of love and care that allows a couple to survive conflict and to grow from criticism.

---

75. Benson, Kyle. "The Magic Relationship Ratio, According to Science." *The Gottman Institute.* October 4, 2017, www.gottman.com/blog/the-magic-relationship-ratio-according-science.

TIMING AND DELIVERY

Okay, we have a loving and positive relationship. Now I need to talk about something I feel should change. A new lethal enemy now appears to me, and it's called urgency. That's the feeling that overcomes us when we think that everything has to be discussed *right now*. The irony is that when it comes to changing myself, I need time and ask for the patience of my spouse. I'll get to it. Slowly, slowly wins the race. But when it comes to something I want her to change about herself, I want it *now*.

From our work with couples, we have found that rarely does a problem demand urgent attention. Urgency is driven by my own heat and emotion and level of upset. It may have little, and usually has no, correlation to the actual timing of when something needs to be said. Of course there are exceptions where outcomes may vary greatly it we don't correct something in the moment ("honey, I think you should move out of the way of the oncoming bus"), but more often than not, the anger and upset and volume that accompany the urgency will more than offset any positive impact of the conversation. Her ears have a way of closing when his mouth is loud and twisted in anger.

What does great timing look like?

First, any critical words should follow a shared positive experience, when good energy is flowing. Second, make sure that it's a time when you both have the headspace for the conversation. That means not during working hours, or when the kids are around, or when one of you is tired or not feeling well. Find the right moment, whether it is a day or even a week later.

The longer you wait and allow your emotions to cool, the more clear and precise you'll become with respect to the point that you want to raise. Even better, the longer you wait, the more likely you'll realize that you can actually live with that thing that was driving you up the wall just a few days earlier. So many things that drive us mad in the moment later appear as small inconveniences amidst an overall happy marriage. Time tends to relieve us of the need for the tough conversation altogether.

Should I really say it?

Great, now several days have elapsed. I passed the initial tests and didn't explode immediately, and I've waited for a moment of peace and positivity to bring up my issue. Here are the key questions to ask yourself in preparation:

- Am I speaking with an enemy, or with my partner in creating a happy marriage and loving family?
- Am I sensitive to the fact that this criticism might make him feel broken, all in the name of my desire to see change?
- Will I be implying in a subtle way that I'm basically fine, and only she has a failing?
- Do I appear oblivious to the fact that he may be confronting and working on other issues in his life, and that this particular gripe, though justifiable, may be too much to add to the mix right now?

- Could it be that what he did was just a normal human mistake, rather than an indication of some profoundly negative trend or trait which needs to be addressed before it spins out of control?
- Is this thing really her issue alone, or is it possible that I'm also partly to blame?

How should I say it?

Once all of the preceding boxes have been checked (it really is something that has to be said, I've waited a week, we've got positive energy), how do I make sure that I say it in the right way? Here are the key components that will help my words be heard:

- Body language: non-aggressive, soft. Hold his hand and look into his eyes.
- Tone of voice: as warm and understanding as possible (the opposite of harsh or condescending).
- Treat him like an equal partner in a great endeavor, not an employee or child.
- Show understanding, care and empathy. "I also find it so hard to...", "I know how much you are putting into this, and it's amazing."
- Make it "we." "I think we both agree that we have to figure a way to discipline the kid without crushing him, so maybe we can both work harder to never yell at him."
- Show you're there for her: "What can I do to help?" "I'm totally here for you." "We're in this together."

If you can't approach your spouse in this way, then drop it for now. Your words won't help, and they are much more likely to backfire. If you can rise to the challenge, you may find the most incredible thing happens: you become closer to your spouse in the process. Working as a team through a problem, even though it was identified as a lack that you felt needed attention, can create a powerful feeling of unity and love.

Fighting the good fight

The most pervasive truth we have discovered regarding fighting is this: *nobody ever wins a fight*. If you lose, then you suffer the humiliation of the vanquished. If you win, any short-term boon to the ego and getting your way this time will be more than offset by the sadness, embarrassment and resentment that has been dealt to your spouse. Every victory is ultimately measured by how great the loss was that it created.

As any fight begins to break out, there should be a single goal: to get out of it. Increasing the volume and harshness of tone and words does nothing but prove that no one is listening. The less he listens, the more she raises the volume. The nastier his words, the more defensive she gets. The loss of control that accompanies anger and outburst increases the chances that I'll say something that is way out of bounds and truly hurtful. Those words can be apologized for, but they — and the pain they caused — don't go away. Do everything you can to short-circuit a fight before it spirals.

The Talmud gives a simple but powerful piece of practical

advice to help prevent an argument from getting out of control. The next time you feel a fight coming on, or you feel the urge to chastise or correct your spouse, lower the volume of your voice. Speak softly. A fight that begins with a soft, lowered tone has a much greater chance of coming to a peaceful close. A lowered voice is like the ropes around a boxing ring; it keeps the fight contained in its place.

POST FACTO

Despite all of our best efforts, we know that fights do happen. On those (hopefully rare) occasions, when we fail to snuff it out as it's kindling, the very least we can do is employ two important strategies of damage control. First, make an agreement during good times that we will never go to bed before resolving our dispute and making up. We can either agree to keep talking until we're calm and come to an agreement, however long it takes, or we can express that we love each other and agree to discuss the details tomorrow after we've slept on it and the heat has passed.

Second — and this never fails — learn to say "I'm sorry." And we don't mean just to say "I'm sorry." We mean to *learn* to say it. Learning requires study, focus, practice, repetition, and sometimes a teacher. When you have done nothing wrong, no argument is brewing, feelings are positive, and your ego is not at stake, find something to say that you are sorry about. "I'm sorry for closing the bathroom door this morning a little too loudly. I hope I didn't wake you up." Practicing "I'm sorry" will make it much easier for you to say it when the argument *is* brewing and feelings are not so positive. You will then be able to say it with feeling, and

— this is key — you will be able to say it even when you feel you were right and your spouse was wrong. "I'm sorry" doesn't mean "I was wrong about everything" or "it's my fault" or "I did bad." It means "I regret that this experience hurt you or belittled you, and that I allowed it to cloud my love for you. That was never my intent, and I apologize for letting it happen." You can't lose with that, so train yourself to do it.

Cutting up and cutting down

The simple truth is that the coarse, rough, negative and hurtful speech which the media and entertainment industry has mercilessly and universally subjected us to from an early age has desensitized us to almost any notion of what is appropriate in human relationships in general and marriage in particular. Not only do we fail to recognize what's harmful, we mistake negative for positive. The most entertaining person to have around is the one who is full of sharp comments and insults and jokes about others. We regard such a person as slick and quick, funny and cool.

For a spouse, such speech can be crushing, especially for a woman, especially if it's from her husband, and especially if it's in front of others. In private she may be able to tolerate her husband's onslaught of "jokes" and insults, but in public those jokes about her looks, cooking, intelligence, weight, whatever can cause severe damage to the trust and bond between you, even though she seems to laugh it off. The witty husband who jokes about his wife is mystified when later she shuts down or cries or expresses anger or pain. "But I was only joking!" is the general husbandly response.

Resolving the problem requires understanding the damaging effects of such speech and then working to unlearn ingrained habits. Ask your spouse to help you by pointing out the moments when you cross the boundary of respectful speech and to sit down with you, after the event, to let you know, in a calm and kind way, what hurt. You'll eventually absorb the lesson and you will see positive change in the way you relate.

PRACTICAL STEPS

We've spent a good deal of ink on the importance of respecting your spouse, the need to build the other through positive speech and through spending, to avoid criticism and cutting down, and to treat the other as the most important person in your world, always. Having tackled some of the large scale issues and challenges, let's turn to some more practical and definable, but nonetheless important, areas of attention and focus.

MY ONE AND ONLY

Never, never ever, speak about past relationships. Men and women (and women in particular) have a way of asking, in tender moments, all snuggled up together, about your first love, your old girlfriends, your past flings. Never, never ever.... Why not? Because at the very least, nothing good will come of it. What could the possible upside be? Openness? Sharing? There are many other things that spouses can share about their pasts — just about everything, really — without speaking about this. It's hard to imagine a scenario in which it would strengthen the relationship to know that there were others. At the very best, it's a neutral. At worst, creating the mental picture and thoughts of prior holders of the spouse's unique and intimate role can create a new insecurity, a new emotional gap. An investor never buys a stock with lots of downside and no upside; telling your spouse about your past relationships is like that stock. We aren't suggesting lying, rather a response that has only upside: "There's no reason to talk about the past. You're my future. And you're the only one I've ever loved."

Oldies but goodies

Did you ever watch an old movie and notice the formality and politeness and manners? The men put on hats before going out and took them off when introduced to a woman. They bowed, and held her chair for her as she was sitting down, then nudged it closer to the table to optimize her comfort. Some of it is comical to us, like putting his coat over the puddle so she can walk across it. But the reality is that good manners with a touch of formality are always a hit with your spouse. Do an experiment: The next time the two of you dine at a restaurant or have a drink at a cafe, when your wife excuses herself to use the ladies' room and returns to the table, instead of looking up from your texting to acknowledge her return, stand up for her and wait for her to sit down before you sit down. Try this one: Hold the door for her as you enter a building. How about opening the car door for her — whether she's the driver or passenger does not matter, nor is there a difference between getting into the car or out. Do you think she'd be offended? At the very worst, she'll think you're being a bit anachronistic and cute and funny (and certainly memorable). At best she'll find it chivalrous, thoughtful and touching, something to make her feel special. This is the kind of stock we love to buy: zero downside and infinite upside.

DON'T BE SECRETIVE

The complexity and wired nature of modern living means that the average person inhabits many worlds. Think about it. We each go to work and inhabit a whole universe of colleagues and contacts with whom we may spend far more time than we spend with our spouse. Making life more complex, we inhabit private worlds even within the limits of the home. My email, and especially my social media, present arenas in which I reside that also separate me from my spouse. The extent to which they're secret is the extent to which my spouse correctly feels shut out of my world. We advise all our students to make sure that their lives are as transparent to their spouses as possible, that they neither hide, nor appear to hide, private lives outside of the marriage. The practical implementation means sharing your passwords to all your accounts. Clearly, if you're an investment banker working on secretive deals, a lawyer or other professional with confidentiality codes, you'll have to keep the work email private. But why should my spouse have to live with the concern that something slightly off color is happening behind the firewall of my social media account or personal email? Showing my spouse that I trust him or her conveys the deepest show of respect.

Along the same lines, my calendar and whereabouts should never be a subject of mystery to my spouse. A husband

and wife should feel accountable for where they are, especially outside of work hours, but even within. Always let him know where you're going, and when you'll be back and what you're up to. Never leave her sitting at home wondering when you're coming home. If you say you'll be back at 10 P.M. and something comes up, call and tell her. Respect means making sure that I never leave my other half in the dark about what I'm doing, thereby ensuring that I never cause any worry or suspicion. When Tod was a young stock analyst, he was instructed that in his business, it wasn't sufficient to act in a way that was legal and appropriate; he also had to always avoid even the "appearance of impropriety." If that's true in the marketplace, how much more is it true in the home. Accountability and transparency will do nothing but build trust, security and love.

Eminent domains

Once upon a time the roles of husbands and wives and mommies and daddies were neatly defined. Think "Leave it to Beaver." We think of those days as sort of *quaint*. But we may yet draw a critical lesson from those bygone days: Domains need to be agreed upon and utterly respected. Few things slowly erode our feelings of worth and competence than having someone constantly sticking their nose in our business with helpful suggestions of how to do things better and tastier and more efficiently. It weakens us, bothers us, makes us feel underappreciated or criticized.

In more traditional environments, domains tend to have default settings, such as she runs the home and has primary responsibility for the children, and he's the breadwinner.

But like all default settings, assignment of domains — areas where either she or he takes primary responsibility — can be changed by common agreement. There are plenty of homes in which he's a better and more passionate cook and she is far better suited to serve as the primary breadwinner and checkbook balancer. The main point is not to push anyone into domains they don't want or aren't suited for, but to make sure that domains are defined and respected. By doing this you'll avoid many unnecessary fights and a lot of hurt feelings, thereby fortifying the relationship in a constant and subtle fashion.

Here are some of the key areas where having a defined role is important:

- *Finances.* While money may or may not be the root of all evil, it surely lies at the center of a disproportionate amount of family stress and tension. Setting this domain is the most surefire way to take that heat down to its coolest possible level. Even if you're both working, figure out who is more willing and more suited to running the family books, making and tending to investments, paying the bills and, yes, balancing the checkbook. You'll avoid many collisions this way. Keep in mind, however, that major financial decisions — the type that involve taking risks or optimizing between saving and spending — should never be made unilaterally. Even if she is the money person in the house, he needs to be consulted regarding the pros and cons of any significant monetary issue.

- *Children.* How do we dress them? When do we let them stay home with the sniffles and when do we push them to go to school? Is homework time enforced? Under what penalty? How much allowance do we give them, and when do we take it away? How late do they stay out? Anyone who has kids knows the almost infinitely broad set of decisions that have to be made over the course of a given week or day. Someone needs to take primary responsibility. Otherwise, every time there's an early pickup, we'll have to fight about whose job is more important. Each judgment call will be a new opportunity for me to second-guess her. Yes, of course, each side remains a parent and a responsible party, and both need to share in the logistics to help each other with their burdens, and any real decisions need to be discussed and agreed upon. Yet primary responsibility needs to be taken and respected and not second-guessed.

- *The kitchen.* Unless they specifically ask, nobody likes it when they're cooking up a dish and someone sticks his (or her) finger into it and says it needs more salt. Grant primary authority over this seemingly innocuous, but important, area of the home, and respect it. That doesn't mean that you can't agree that every Tuesday night she takes over his kitchen and makes Chinese (in which case he has to stay out). But it does mean that apart from that midweek role-change, she allows him to do his thing. Oh, and we must not forget to mention that in our opinion, dishes are always a shared job.

- *Home furnishings and decor.* Although this, too, seems like a trivial issue, it is not. How we'll decorate the home, selection and placement of the furniture, where we hang the paintings, and which ones we hang, and, when it's time to throw out his beloved college-days recliner — all of those decisions should be placed into the domain of one of the partners. Often it's the one who spends more time in the home and thus deserves to make it more comfortable for themselves. Other times, we'll agree that one or the other of us really has much better taste. As in other domains, any major decisions, especially those involving significant financial outlay, must involve both parties.

DICTATORSHIP

Taking primary responsibility for a certain domain does not imply that you are free to become a dictator. To the contrary, basic respect and kindness mandate frequently asking your spouse for their opinion and input. You may or may not choose to incorporate the suggestion, but it always shows that you care about their feelings and sensitivities. The intention behind delegating domains is not to create absolute power in the hands of any particular party, but rather to make sure that we respect boundaries and build and enable our spouse in areas where they are most willing or suited to express themselves.

202 ❧ NOT A PARTNERSHIP

PILLAR #4:
It All Depends On Me

CHANGE THE GAME

Many of us enter marriage looking forward to the many benefits that await us. Love, intimacy, trust, support, shared times. Few of us look to marriage as the primary arena in which we have both an opportunity and, dare we say, *obligation* to work on perfecting our character. This is arguably, if not clearly, the most noble calling and goal to which a human can aspire. If we could sum up the job of a spouse in one single overarching idea, it would go as follows: I need to work on becoming the husband (or wife) that my spouse needs me to be.

That leads to another option in the process of trying to make my marriage flourish: *What if I just focus on improving myself?*

You mean she's *not* the problem?

In case you think that focusing on yourself somehow doesn't apply to you, just ask yourself the following question about the thing that bothers you most about your spouse (for example, my spouse is occasionally cold and uncaring): *Was he or she like this when we got married?* If the answer is yes, then you'll need to ask yourself a follow-up question about why you married him or her in the first place! More likely, the answer to the first question is, hmm, not really. I remember her as quite warm and always concerned.

In that case, question two is: *What might **I** have done to cause her to become cold and uncaring?*

Take it upon yourself

One of the most powerful ways to give to my spouse is by taking responsibility for dealing with my own core issues. We sometimes incorrectly define this type of personal work as lying *outside* of the marriage (since it's just about me), but nothing could be further from the truth, especially when the motivation is to become a better spouse.

We often learn this truth the hard way. Take, for example, a needy husband. He looks at his wife a few years into the relationship and says: "She is cold and uncaring" — and that's that. "I'll find another woman who can express the warmth and nurture I so crave." How does that work out in practice? According to author and marital therapist Michele Weiner-Davis, "Although it's true that some people learn from their mistakes in their first marriages and are able to develop happier second marriages, by no means is this the rule. In fact, sixty percent of second marriages end in divorce! One of the reasons there are more divorces in second marriages is that people enter their second marriages with the bad relationship habits they learned the first time around. They simply find new partners with whom they can do that old familiar dance."[76]

We often exacerbate the problems caused by our own unresolved issues when we cling to the superficial belief that marriage will provide the magic elixir to cure our unhappiness. So rather than working to build happiness through our growth and work as individuals and as a couple, we assume it's just my crummy partner's fault. Concludes Weiner-Davis: "If you are of the belief that marriage should make you happy, then you will undoubtedly start to think something major is lacking in your spouse and that you should get out of your marriage. The problem is, unless you feel satisfied with your own life, you will not be able to decipher whether your unhappiness stems from personal or relationship issues. If you jump to conclusions and assume you need to dump your partner and try another, you are likely to be sorely disappointed because you will find yourself in the same state of unhappiness. Your next marriage won't cure the unhappiness problem either."[77]

CHOICE OF SPOUSE

Marriage flows and sparkles when both spouses push for greater levels of giving, understanding and nurturing. It falters when each side is out for himself or herself. But here's the *aha*: you have the power to build your marriage irrespective

---

76. Weiner-Davis, Michele. "Relationship IQ Quiz." *Divorce Busting*. 2009, divorcebusting.com/a_relationship_iq_quiz.htm.
77. Weiner-Davis, M.

of whether your spouse is playing their role properly. It's a choice. We have seen countless marriages saved and nursed back to health after just one or the other has said "*I* am going to make it happen," and then started to do so.

From the standpoint of each of you, it's the most powerful opportunity that exists in marriage. I can choose to fix my relationship, to start the process, to look at the responsibility as being *all mine*. Or I can take the easy way out and say it is simply out of my hands; it's up to the other. How many times have we heard a spouse say: "I just can't handle it anymore. He has to change!" That translates roughly to: "I have tried and worked to the limit of my capacity. Doing more is beyond me. From here on, I demand that he change instead!" Which itself can be read as: "I'm no longer responsible. He is."

THE BLAME GAME

When it comes to change, especially in our marriages, we all too often start with our spouse. If only he or she would improve, we think, our relationship and life together would be so much better. Most of us are expert diagnosticians when it comes to locating the problems that other people need to work on. Even in situations where we can pinpoint difficult external circumstances that are causing stress — work or health or children issues — we may often believe that things would not be so bad if our spouse would just do x or y or z.

We see this dynamic frequently in our own work with couples. We have also heard through our almost constant interaction with marital therapists that the major agenda couples take into the therapy office is exactly this: "I want my spouse to change!"

Why is this attitude so commonplace among spouses? According to researchers at the Gottman Institute, "Blaming provides us with a means to discharge our pain, and makes us feel as though we have some grasp of control on a negative situation. While it may feel good to release anger by blaming others, it hurts our relationships." In the words of author Brene Brown, "blaming has an inverse relationship with accountability."[78]

Exacerbating the problem still further, we often lack the maturity and tolerance to handle anything less than perfection. More accurately, we can *endlessly* tolerate less than perfect behavior in ourselves. After all, it's part of my emotional make-up, a product of my dysfunctional parents, it's complicated and deep, it takes time.... At the same time we show little patience for the faults of other. That's why we tend to demand immediate and often out-of-reach change from others, and especially from our spouse. Simply put, it's always easier to point a finger than to lift one.

START WITH *YOU*

While taking responsibility for my own contributions to marital disharmony can challenge even the best of us, it offers the most hope for two reasons. First, the leverage is substantial: curing a recurrent character flaw that is poisoning my marriage (and usually my job and other relationships) is *the* quintessential game changer. Second, and equally

---

78. Sangwin, Becca. "Why We Need to Stop Playing the Blame Game." *The Gottman Institute.* May 19, 2016, www.gottman.com/blog/why-we-need-to-stop-playing-the-blame-game.

important, it is squarely in *my hands* to make it happen. Many people who work hard on their marriages end up frustrated and resentful since too often they perceive (sometimes correctly) that the spouse isn't equally invested in the work. Real marital improvement begins with the axiom that if I can fix myself, my marriage will improve right alongside me. Our experience shows that such actions almost always drive the additional benefit of inspiring the spouse to work harder as well.

That simply-expressed insight — *it's up to me!* — holds the key to all change and improvement. In the words of psychotherapist and marriage counselor Mel Schwartz, "You can't change an other, but, by changing yourself, the energy of the relationship shifts and makes it easier for the other person to correspond. Relationships are, at the core, informed by the energy of the relationship — simply how you each feel about each other, more than an 'objective' truth. You can shift the energy by going first. When you modify or alter your attitude or communication, the other party is now in a different relationship. If you change yourself, they must be affected."[79]

Many great thinkers have stressed that change depends upon me. Mahatma Gandhi put it this way: "Be the change that you wish to see in the world." That succinct call to action echoes an insight of the leading Jewish ethicist of the 19th century: "At first I tried to change the world, and I failed. Then I tried to change my city, and I failed. Then

---

79. Schwartz, Mel. "Be the Change You Ask for in Others." *Psychology Today.* November 17, 2014, www.psychologytoday.com/us/blog/shift-mind/201411/be-the-change-you-ask-in-others.

I tried to change my family, and I failed. Finally, I tried to change myself, and then I was able to change the world."[80]

When we apply these concepts to marriage, we are on our way to happiness and fulfillment in the relationship.

THE BENEFITS

Taking responsibility for improving my marriage can rapidly cascade into a range of related positive outcomes. For example, my growing sense of accountability will often allow me, finally, to stop demanding and expecting change in my spouse. The moment I lower those expectations, my patience increases concomitantly. (In fact, what are expectations, other than a creation of my own mind that give me permission to be disappointed every time they're not met?) That means fewer disappointments and less and less blame. That in turn produces more marital harmony.

That's just my side. The bonus rounds occur as my spouse begins to react in a number of likely ways. First, he or she may feel a new sense of ease and peace as I spend less time judging and expecting. Her growing realization that I'm happy and satisfied with her as she is will empower her and enhance her sense of worth and well-being. Positive feelings in turn give her the energy and incentive to seek out ways of contributing herself. She may also be inspired by the work I'm doing on myself, given the fact that she'll be the direct beneficiary, to begin reciprocating with new levels of improvement and self-control on her end. That positive feedback will only encourage me to do more.

---

80. Rabbi Yisrael Salanter.

Build it and it will come

Great marriages don't happen; we build them. The greatness of a spouse is measured by the extent to which he or she pushes the boundaries of responsibility, never abandoning the ability to choose and act. I can always make it better, irrespective of what my spouse does. It all depends on me. With this attitude, a husband or wife can literally save the marriage. When *both* spouses take responsibility, marriage isn't only saved, it blossoms. It sparkles. Don't confuse this with a mythical union of perfection and lack of conflict. To the contrary, taking responsibility for an *imperfect* marriage between two *imperfect* people is the way to work through conflict in order to build a beautiful and attainable relationship.

"Blame game" to "game on!"

Okay, I got it. It's up to me. Now what? How do I begin to focus on taking the necessary steps to make things better? What does that look like in practical terms?

Let's break this call to battle into two primary plans of action:

1. *Figure out what I can do to improve my own behavior and character*, including my ability not only to tolerate, but to *embrace*, my spouse, despite his or her shortcomings. This means working on myself — my character and blockages, not just my abs! — with all my energy.

2. *Learn to self-regulate.* This means taking responsibility for and control of my thoughts, feelings and responses. Remember, none of us has the right to respond whenever and however we see fit.

Plan #1: Work on my own issues

GET OUT OF YOURSELF BY GETTING **IN** TO YOURSELF

No one enters marriage with a clean slate. All the personal issues, insecurities, bad character traits, and liabilities I suffered from when I was single, often from childhood, follow me right into my marriage. We each have certain core issues (like laziness or tendency to anger) that manifest themselves in all aspects of our lives, albeit clothed in different guises. Rather than creating new issues, then, marriage tends to create yet another forum for those pre-existing issues to express themselves, but often without the accompanying self-control we exert in other areas of life, such as work.

For example, a person who hates feeling "controlled" will find it irritating when his boss or colleague at work asks him to perform a task that he feels is beneath him, or is someone else's responsibility. In the professional environment he'll control himself mightily, lest it reflect badly upon him. When his accountant — who works for him — asks too many questions or demands some unpleasant action, he'll be *somewhat less* controlled; after all, he's the client!

When it comes to his wife, whom he may well take for granted and feel *belongs* to him, should she ask him to take out the garbage again or fail to say please, he may well erupt in rage. All the more so if he was harboring frustration from those other violations in the workplace, for which the spouse must now, quite unfairly, pay. In his mind, it's all about his controlling spouse. In reality, it's about an unresolved character issue that may trace itself back to a controlling mother or father that has now found one more corrosive place for expression.

The husband's reactions in such cases may over time wear his wife out to the point where she begins to shut down and pull away. He sees the reaction as unrelated to any of his own causative issues, and thus curses his sad fate for delivering him a cold, demanding and uncaring wife, never realizing that he brought about the outcome himself, or at the very least contributed to it.

MARITAL MATH

It follows, then, that whatever we don't fix before marriage comes right into the relationship with us, like pieces of old, non-matching furniture. Add hers to mine and then multiply by all the combinations and permutations that the intertwined relationship presents, and, *whoa*, we've created a highly explosive chemical reaction! In the moment, lacking control, we'll blame, become indignant, or say hurtful things (that never get forgotten, as every spouse knows). We might, upon cooling down, have the dignity to forgive or to say I'm sorry, but as long as the poisonous root is still in place the weeds and thorns will keep popping up in the garden of our marriage. The tragedy is that it winds up being the same fights, sometimes in different guises and sometimes just a repeat, for years on end.

The funny thing is that beneath all the facades we present in the various roles we play, most of us are relatively simple and straightforward when it comes to our positive and negative attributes. But as life rolls on and becomes ever more complicated and "noisy," we lose track of ourselves amidst the chaos and turmoil. We spend our days trying in futility to quiet the noise or control the complexity, all the while ignoring the core issues that hold us back.

Just think for a moment about what your life would look like if you could begin to rid yourself of *just one* negative trait, such as anger or hypersensitivity or laziness. Consider the incredible impact that could have on every aspect of your life, and none more than your marriage. In fact, the moment I stop blaming my partner for my unhappiness and instead begin to focus on my own character and behavior, everything begins to change.

JUST ASK

There's a great story told about a guy who goes out on his first date with a woman and begins talking about himself and talking about himself and talking about himself. After about an hour of this, he finally turns to her and says: "Okay — enough about me! What do *you* think of me?"

Anyone facing difficulty identifying his or her character flaws need only ask his spouse or friends or parents with an open heart. Start with the question: What is it really like to be around me, to interact with me, to be my friend, my colleague, my spouse? That identification process, while painful, can be incredibly enlightening if you truly give someone you trust and who knows you permission to answer honestly (and, hopefully, with sensitivity).

Once identified, now it's time to actually start the work of improving. When it comes to the practical steps we can take to fix a character flaw, there are endless numbers of books, support groups and therapists out there. Those processes lie beyond the purview of this book to explore in any depth. Our objective here is to change your *mindset* — to help you to realize that it's in your hands to change yourself and your marriage, and that the time to begin the work of improving is right now!

The real question is: How badly do you want to do it? Once you take the difficult step of resolving yourself to take responsibility and begin the work — irrespective of whether your spouse is working alongside you — you will figure out the "how to" without a problem. A coach, a therapist, some deep dives into research on character improvement — your desire to change will lead you to the right resources.

But if you don't truly want to change yourself, and you can't really stand behind the work, then no amount of reading, studying or therapy will help. You will find yourself talking about change until your proverbial face turns blue, yet with pitifully inadequate results.

What are you waiting for? It's all in your hands!

Plan #2: Self-regulate

Not surprisingly, the character-trait changes of Plan #1 take time to implement. We can't uproot patterns that formed over decades in a few weeks or months. It will take patience and work (so by all means get started now!). Plan #2, while not totally separable from Plan #1, may nonetheless produce somewhat more immediate results. This strategy goes by a few different names — exercising free will, self-regulation, restraint — but whatever you want to call it, it leads to increased self-control in marital interactions in the moment. Let's explore this incredibly fertile ground for human expression and relationship building.

FREE WILL(Y)

Much of our success and failure in life depends on whether and how we use our free will. The choices we make determine who we are and what we are. When we speak of free will, we're not referring to the sometimes painful choice between vanilla and chocolate ice cream. That's merely a tallying up of taste bud stimulation. True free will is exercised when we choose between *two worlds*, between my lower, self-centered and physically-oriented self, and my higher, giving, nurturing, other-oriented self. Said another way, it's when we struggle to do *what we know* is the right thing rather than taking the easy route. It exists solely in the realm of ethical (or moral or spiritual — whatever term you prefer) decisions.

It leads us either *to*, or *away* from, that life we so badly want to live. If we focus for a moment on what we dream our kids will say about us when they give our eulogies, more than likely we hope they'll talk about the way we chose to live by the values and nobility of our conscience rather than the expediencies of our cravings.

We act in our highest and most uniquely human capacity when we exercise free will to grow and to build ourselves and others. The actions we've been trained for, practiced, made perfect, and now do by rote are not the products of my current free will, but of habit. Interestingly, even many of the positive things I do may not actually reflect a moral victory on my part. To the contrary, they may just flow from the great training my parents provided rather than a current free will struggle.

Nor can we choose to act in ways that lie too far beyond our reach. Real choice is pitched right at that point where we can either *choose* to go forward with effort and grow, or to simply take the path of least resistance and shrink. Failure to choose is itself a choice. It diminishes us and shifts our responsibility onto others.

Boss vs. loss

Lest you think free-will decision making is a dramatic and occasional event, just think about the choices you'll make over the course of any given day. At lunch, do I order the burger and fries I so crave, or make do with a salad? Think about that choice for a moment. It seems like a trivial matter, but in reality it reflects a far deeper battle between my longer term vision for myself (slim, healthy, energetic, alive...) and my desire for a short-term pleasure that may override that bigger goal. Let's say I'm looking for a job. Do I get up early or stay in bed another hour? Again, it's the longer term vision versus the shorter term pleasure. Oh, by the way, the longer term goal — which holds the promise for the greatest pleasure and well-being — frequently loses to the fantasy held out by our lower self, which craves and can provide the transient benefit *right now*. Such dilemmas confront us all day long.

When we turn from these more or less personal choices to the exercise of self-control in our relationships, it gets a bit trickier. When faced with a decision to make in the context of relationships, we tend to distinguish between interactions with immediate or severe consequences and those where we can pretty much get away with it. Let's say someone insults me or speaks down to me. How will I react? The answer depends on who did the insulting. If it was my boss, I'll probably begrudgingly accept it; for sure I won't strike back. The resulting loss of my job or likelihood of getting passed over for a raise is ever on my mind and keeps me in check. If it was my colleague, more of an equal, it could go either way. But, usually, my professionalism will triumph in the work setting, and I'll either let it go or perhaps gain control of myself and then calmly approach the offending person with my grievance.

BUT NOT AT HOME!

Now, let's say it was my wife or husband who spoke down to me. First, it hurts more, since the respect I need and want from my spouse is so much more a part of my well-being, and it presents a bigger departure from my expectations. Second, the consequence of letting fly are significantly lower *in the moment*. So, I'll let her have it!

Now place that interaction into the context of free will and self-restraint. What will happen to our relationship? Longer term, especially when losing control and lashing out happen frequently, the consequences can be staggering. More than in any other arena, my decision to exercise self-control in marriage can be described as nothing less than make or break. The bitter irony is that the short-term pleasure here is a *nothing*. What do I gain, even in the moment, from striking back against my spouse? A momentary feeling of control? Regaining of my pride and sense of self? To the contrary, anyone with a modicum of humanity or sensitivity will be left feeling empty and worthless. The more strongly I silence her, the more decisively I win a marital fight, the more I have in fact lost.

At least the burger gives me a moment of real pleasure.

TOGETHER...

Our marital interactions, whether generic or dramatic, occur on almost a moment by moment basis when we're together. They are split between doing and restraining.

For example, do I make sure to...

- ...smile at her when I see her or continue brooding over whatever is bothering me?
- ...spend time talking to him even though I want to start exercising?
- ...put my phone on silent at dinner in order to fully focus on my spouse?
- ...speak with total respect?

And am I able to hold myself back and not...

- ...mention everything that bothers me?
- ...make that sly or cutting comment?
- ...speak in a condescending manner?
- ...make that facial expression of frustration?

Assuming that our answers to those basic questions made us cringe, we're faced with another question: Exactly where did the notion come from that when we come home, or when we deal with our spouses in general, we have the right to stop self-regulating?

Well, I need someplace to be myself, to let it all hang out, to let my guard down, right?

Wrong. Of course, our marriages and homes need to provide safety, comfort and a relaxed environment. But that does not translate into an allowance to speak and act however I want with my spouse. Much of the self-control we demonstrate in the public sphere has to be carried over into the private domain. Why should my colleagues get the best of me and my wife the worst?

We heard a first-hand story about a famous rabbi in his 80s who was helping a friend of ours on an educational project that ran all day and well into the evening. When our friend dropped off the rabbi in front of his house, he saw the most extraordinary thing take place. The distinguished elder literally *ran* to his front door so as not to leave his wife waiting a single moment more than was necessary once his work ended. Then, just before he gave a little knock (so as to not startle her) and entered, he straightened his tie, buttoned his jacket and readied himself like a teenager wanting to make a good impression on his prom date. Only then did he enter his home. We can be pretty sure that, once inside, before he sat down to dinner, he spoke kindly with his wife and asked her about her day.

Observing this amazing person reminded us that one's wife is entitled to the best of him, not a spent, tired, unkempt and unguarded version. It was free will and self-regulation in action!

...And apart

Even when we're apart, perhaps especially then, I'll be faced with decisions that affect my spouse and the long-term health of the relationship. It is widely believed that as many as 85% of extramarital affairs begin in the workplace.[81] Why? Well, for one thing, both we and our co-workers present our absolute best in the workplace. We smell good, look good, wear our most attractive clothing, and, of course, we always speak and act with control and calculation. Secondly, the workplace simply presents the greatest number of opportunities to step beyond appropriate behaviors, to flirt or text or share a bit too much. Within that cluster, business trips present the most intense challenges to fidelity,[82] given the wicked combination of loneliness and the likelihood of getting away with it. Online dalliances have also begun to take center stage in destroying the protective boundaries to our emotional and physical intimacy.

These scenarios play out daily in our private and work lives, forcing us to choose the world we wish to embrace. Fulfilling myself outside of marriage pits the moral, ethical and loyalty aspects of my heart and soul directly against the lower, physical, pleasure-seeking interests of my body. To the extent that I feel my emotional needs unmet within the marriage, my heart may well defect to the side of the body when the opportunity to cheat presents itself.

---

81. Hollander, Lori. "Five Truths Every Married Person Needs to Know about Affairs." *Good Therapy*. July 21, 2011, www.goodtherapy.org/blog/truths-workplace-affair.
82. Lehnardt, Karin. "64 Interesting Facts about Affairs." *Fact Retriever*. December 26, 2016, www.factretriever.com/affairs-facts.

So whether at home or at work, with issues that are personal, professional or relate directly to my marital relationships, there's simply no way around it. I either have to exercise free will to connect to my higher self with all my strength, or cede myself, and often my marriage, to short-term pleasure and expediency.

PRACTICAL STEPS

There is no way around it. Self-restraint takes practice. It's not much different from learning to hit a backhand. You have to do it over and over again until it becomes muscle memory. Similar to what we noted regarding character-trait improvement, a little bit of research will reveal endless pathways to learning the steps.

In the meanwhile, we'd also suggest the following. Try to focus initially — starting today — on just one interaction per day outside of your marriage where what you feel like doing is pitted against what you know is the right thing to do. For example, your Mom is calling and you stare at the phone, hoping she knows you probably are busy with a colleague...but you answer and say, "Hi Mom! I'm so happy to hear from you!" Or, back to our lunch example, despite that heavenly aroma of sauteed onions and barbeque beef coming from the guy's plate at the table right next to you, boldly go for the chicken salad with light vinaigrette. Spend a full week focusing just once a day on making a good, free-will decision. See how amazing it feels to gain control of yourself.

There's a second exercise we also suggest implementing today, this one inside your marriage. Following in the footsteps of that aforementioned rabbi, before you walk through your front door tonight, take 20 seconds and focus on the initial greeting that you will give your spouse. Ask yourself: What does he deserve right now? What is the right way to greet her? Then make a choice and make it happen. Pay attention to the response. Try to implement this with more thought and more follow-through across the course of the next week (and thereafter).

Parenthetically, research in the field of positive psychology has provided ample evidence that gaining control over how we make choices has a significant impact on our self-esteem, well-being and happiness. Imagine the spillover effect for your spouse as he or she begins interacting ever more with a happy, fulfilled and self-respecting version of you.

Conclusion

In this book we have tried to provide you with a more clear definition of what marriage is, and why it's worth doing the work to make it great. We've also attempted to dispel some of the myths and fantasies that pollute our thinking and knock us off course in our journey to attaining a strong relationship.

A high-functioning marriage can merge two quite different individuals into a new unified entity. A great marriage provides strength, happiness, security, satisfaction and well-being to both partners. It won't happen by itself, it isn't easy, and you can't get there by taking. It's all about what you give. When you become the type of husband or wife your spouse needs you to be, the relationship will blossom. Through giving, you'll find the pathway to becoming the greatest, most powerful version of yourself possible. The greater you are, the more your marriage will flourish.

When your marriage flourishes, *you* will be the ultimate beneficiary. It's a reality, not a ruse. When you give to your spouse, he or she will begin to open up and give back. That response will in turn provide more energy for more giving on your part, and so on. You'll become more of a pleasure to be around. More loving. More reliable. That will put your spouse at ease and create a deeper sense of well-being. A growing sense of happiness and security will generate a flow of love right back to you. Once you spark that natural response system, the marriage will take flight, lifting both spouses along with it. It is one of life's great, *if not greatest*, virtuous cycles.

Our second objective was to compact the concept of giving — which can be a part of literally every point of contact with your spouse — into a manageable structure of four pillars. Over the course of your marriage you will need to master all four: keeping it fresh, expressing gratitude, showing respect and taking responsibility.

We all know that we can't work on everything at once. The key is to be constantly at work on one pillar or another. Do it alone. Do it together. Make it a project for date nights. When you feel stale in one area, move to another. When you finish the cycle, restart it. Deepen it. Just keep going.

There it is. You are now armed with a clear picture of what healthy marriage looks like, and the tools to make it happen. The main thing is to start the work. As the famous Jewish maxim states: If not now, *when*? Start the journey today that will bring you and your spouse to the place of true marital bliss.

Acknowledgments

BEFORE WE DARED TO RAISE pen to paper on such a misunderstood and complex a subject as marriage, we had to first spend two or three decades learning, living and experiencing the building of our own marriages and families. We also needed an overlapping decade and a half or so of teaching, observing and counseling our students to develop a real world perspective on where and how the theories could be applied to help others. While we surely could use more time and experience tweaking and testing the theories, the desperate state of marriage today outweighs our caution. Thus, as the adage (sort of) goes, we decided to cease fishing and cut bait.

Those decades of learning about marriage happened only because we had great teachers. Our debt of gratitude to them cannot be fully expressed, but a few standouts must be mentioned. In the world of Jewish thought, the written works of R. C. Friedlander and R. E. E. Dessler brought to light both mystical and practical marital wisdom. These works were further honed, adapted and expressed by three of our own teachers and mentors, Beryl Gershenfeld, Aharon Lopiansky and Dr. Akiva Tatz — the latter of whose fingerprints are to be found throughout this book (and indeed his lectures and writings on marriage, among other topics, are treasure troves). We also acknowledge the role that one of the most esteemed Jewish thinkers and leaders of this generation, Rabbi Aharon Feldman, played by encouraging us to take on this project.

In the world of contemporary marital academia and research, we owe our thanks to the enlightening work and insight of Dr. Martin Seligman at the University of Pennsylvania, the founder of Positive Psychology. Our thinking and knowledge have been deeply affected by his teaching and research, and through direct and indirect encounters with him and many of his students.

The book itself has been endlessly stress-tested and improved by the expert help of our team of editors and colleagues, Joseph Shaw, Jonathan Taub, and a dear and dedicated student, Kenny Wallach. The artwork and design belong to our talented student Jared Schwartz, while Zach Horwitz and Ben Weber have invested themselves heavily to help us bring the written word to the broader world.

The true heroes of our endeavors are the hundreds of students who have passed through our institute. The relationships begin with our taking the role of teacher and counselor, but ultimately we become students of their experiences and struggles to build beautiful marriages and families. Those ongoing encounters have been endlessly enriching and we are fortunate to be a part of their lives.

Lastly, we acknowledge the truest and deepest debt of gratitude to our wives and families, who have provided each of us with the love, encouragement and, yes, partnership, that has sustained our respective families and has enabled any and all work that we have been fortunate to produce.